To Oli
with

My Life Has
Been Blessed

and my love

Anne

My Life Has Been Blessed

Anne Ritchie

Bannister Publications Ltd
118 Saltergate
Chesterfield
Derbyshire S40 1NG

First published in Great Britain in 2011 by

Bannister Publications Ltd
118 Saltergate
Chesterfield
Derbyshire S40 1NG

Copyright © Anne Ritchie

ISBN 978-0-9566196-7-9

Anne Ritchie asserts her moral right
to be identified as the author of this work

A catalogue record for this book is available from the British Library

Set in Palatino Linotype and cover design by
Escritor Design, Chesterfield, Derbyshire

Printed and bound in the UK by the MPG Books Group,
Bodmin and King's Lynn

For the love of my family, Gilbert, Adele and Craig and my brother George, sisters Jenny and Ellen, who through lots of humour have helped me through good times and bad. For Sylvia, who is a dear friend and a wonderful musician and for the fun we have. I have so many wonderful friends that if I mentioned them by name, I'm sure to miss someone out - they know who they are. Most of all I have the love of God in my heart and that I will cherish always.

Shortly after completing this book, Ellen's dear husband, Graham, died and he is sorely missed.

Chapter 1

From the title it would appear that my life is one of constant laughter and fun, but just like everyone else in this world I have had many ups and downs some major some minor, but through it all I always felt that I would get through each one; I didn't know how or why, but somewhere in deep inside I knew. I do hope that you will read on and discover how I feel my life *has* been blessed.

I was born in the slums of Glasgow just after the war. I hate to admit even that as everyone can now work out my age. I still feel eighteen inside, but not when I look in the mirror, thinking to myself, I didn't know Mum was visiting. I was brought up in a condemned tenement in a place called Govan. It was very near the shipyards and from our windows we could see the ships being built in the distance. At New Year, even as a child, I was always touched by the mournful sounds of the horns of the ships when twelve o'clock sounded.

It was a very grey place with lots of industrial works around and I remember looking into a huge grey building as far as I can remember, with no windows. It was called the Thermotank and I haven't a clue what they made but it was a very imposing building. There were also Harland and Wolf and Polar Engines near our house and apparently the Luftwaffe missed both of these and hit the football field nearby, much to the dismay of the keen footballers.

What I recall of the street I lived on was that the roads were very smooth, which made them ideal for every sort of game, including football and roller skating. The boys made a sort of cart thing from an old box and wheels from an old pram, and decorated with bottle tops, in which they sped up and down the roads with great glee. Football was a memorable game, in that there would be about twenty men on each side with their shirt sleeves rolled up and braces holding up their trousers. This game was such a favourite in the summer, with the wives of the teamsters leaning out of their windows or 'windae hingin' to shout their 'comments' to their menfolk.

As was the norm then, aunties, uncles and other extended family members lived nearby, so we visited each other regularly and got to know each other very well. My grandmother, who was such a tiny little lady, had five children, the youngest of whom was only six weeks old when her husband died. I cannot imagine how she coped. Apparently she took in washing and went out cleaning, just to make ends meet. They talk about the 'good old days'. I recently learned that she also helped deliver children, and lay out the dead. I learned after my Grandmother had been bereaved, that she approached the local Protestant church to apply for help and was turned down, but she later learned that lots of money had been given to the Catholic Church from the Church that she approached. No wonder that there was still great enmity between Protestants and Catholics.

My Granny always told us that we were to look for the 'Harrower millions'. We were always curious to find out exactly what she meant. Later on my sister Jenny was tracing our family tree, and she found a lady called Annie Harrower. We later found out that my great grandfather was a coachman to a grand house. So, maybe my Granny was taken there, thinking that the grand house belonged to someone in our family and perhaps there was a chance that we would inherit the 'Harrower millions'. But it was to no avail, although Jenny and I had great fun imagining how we'd spend it all.

What I remember of my Mum's sisters is not as good as my sister's recollection but I do remember my Auntie Mary, who was an absolute hoot. She was very small, but had a huge sense of humour, which she needed to cope with all her traumas. Strange things would always happen to her, like the time she was painting the ceiling and walked off the end of the table.

She had very small feet and one day when passing a shoe shop, she noticed that a sale was on, so she went in and the assistant, who knew her, said that there were a few sample shoes. They were just her size, Size 3, so she went into the back and came out with a beautiful pair of sandals. Auntie Mary tried them on and realised something was not quite right with the shoes. She looked down and saw that they were both left shoes, as the buckles were on the same side. She pointed this out but was assured by the assistant that for only three shillings, she could get away with them.

She had a very hard time in her marriage, having married a man who was about a foot taller than her. I think this was a bone of contention for him and he always made snide remarks about her height. He would walk far in front of her when they were out, a pointless exercise as they might as well have gone out separately. Despite this, every time we met her we knew that we were in for a good laugh.

My Auntie Jean also had a hard time in her life. She had the most beautiful red hair and Jenny and Ellen told me that when she was younger she looked like Rita Hayworth. She had a job in Stevenson's Shipyard as a Rate Fixer, I think it's called Time and Motion now, and she earned more than the men, which was unheard of in those days. She had the most beautiful clothes and she carried herself really well. She looked a million dollars.

While working at the shipyard, around Christmas time, the joiners would 'take orders' and Jean would come home with wooden school cases and pencil boxes they had made. We often wondered how the Foreman reacted when he found out, but apparently he was the first in line to put in an order! In that same vein, my Granny had been living in a 'single end', a one roomed flat, which was lit by gas. She had electricity installed by Auntie Jean but was so afraid of it that she would only touch the switch when someone was there with her, so no doubt she sat in the dark for many an hour until a visitor arrived.

Auntie Jean had a love affair with a very nice young man who was Catholic – here we go again – and had a baby daughter, Josie, with him, but was not allowed to marry him. She married a very handsome man called James, who was diabetic and unfortunately liked to drink. He made little Josie's life a misery when she was growing up. Auntie Jean had two more children, a girl and a boy, also called James, who was the apple of his father's eye. I was told that Jean's daughter of her first union felt unloved by her stepfather and I suppose she found it difficult to forgive him. Auntie Jenny was very friendly with Jean and befriended her throughout the hard times she must have had and they still correspond with each other. Josie married when she was quite young and she and her husband emigrated to Canada.

When my Auntie Jean was an old lady she found that

a letter had been sent to her son, which contained quite a revelation. The letter stated that the writer was her husband James' son. He explained that James had been in the Army during the war and had had an affair with a lady in Holland. The man said he would like to meet up with his new family and could they book him into a hotel in Glasgow. This was duly done and they met, but Auntie Jean just couldn't cope. I think she must have remembered how badly her husband had treated her daughter , and all the time he had a son by another woman.

Mum told me that she was never the same after this and went into a decline and died in a nursing home a few years later. Mum was quite naturally upset, especially that when they were first married he forbade her to wear make-up or dress up in nice clothes, as she was used to doing before they met. He had a strange hold over her but maybe women could not answer back the way we can now. Anyway he died when he was a relatively young man, around fortyish, so she and her two children lived with my Granny until the old lady died.

Uncle Tommy was also a small chap but I always loved it when he came to visit, as he was always doing magic tricks, amusing us for hours with coins and bits of string. He made a set of cricket stumps for George, but Ellen decided to claim them as she was a bit of a tomboy and I don't think George ever saw them again. At New Year parties he always brought along his accordion, which he played really well.

New Year was a great event and the house would be cleaned from top to bottom. Clean curtains would be hung, paint would be washed down, carpets taken outside and beaten. This was my job when I was old enough and I remember the clouds of dust hovering around my head. At five minutes to twelve the bins would be taken down to the 'midden' so that the house would be spotless to bring in the New Year. Someone with black or dark hair would be asked to be the 'first foot', a supposedly lucky charm, hoping that they would have a lump of coal or a bit of bun for luck. A great big steak pie would be ordered from Bob the butcher, which would be eaten with the usual extras and consumed with great gusto after the 'bells'. I wasn't allowed to stay up until I was older but I remember Mum buying Madeira cake, 'currant bun', and raspberry cordial to be consumed the next day. New Year parties seemed to last forever and I could never sleep for the noise of the revellers.

My Auntie Lizzy was always smiling, which was a miracle since she really had a hard time. Her husband used to beat her, much to my Mum's anger. She told me that she was always ready to tackle him about it, but thought better of it, as Lizzy would probably suffer more for it. Her husband had been in the Merchant Navy and was a particularly strong man, so she was no match for him. Their sons also were beaten regularly until they were old enough to fight back; they took him round to the back court, did what they had to and he never did it again. She had nine children and as a child I always wondered why she was so fat sometimes and thin other times. But through it all she was always smiling and singing little songs. She was like this until the day she died, although I find it difficult to understand as five of her children died before her. Her heart must have been shredded into little pieces.

My Granny had two sisters who were like chalk and cheese. One of them had obviously married very well and lived in a beautiful part of the city. She had lovely 'things' the like of which I had never seen before. I sat in awe in her home every time we visited, too frightened to say anything. She always had her hair in the same style in two long plaits wound round her head, not quite like Princess Leah in Star Wars, but not far off.

The other sister was the complete opposite in that she didn't bother with her appearance and lived alone with her cats. I never really knew her and mostly only saw her from a distance. According to my sisters that was just as well. This aunt, Jemima, seemed a very strange woman, always scruffy and I was always afraid of her. She had a 'friend' who we did not see very often, fortunately, but when we met at Granny's house I was always plonked on this lady's knee and I remember the thick dark make-up caked on to her face, doing nothing to conceal the lines, and she was drenched in the perfume 'Evening in Paris'. She lived in London and there was always whispering when she left, as people those days thought that Londoners lived in another world. Jenny recalls many times when she was dragged down to the coast with Aunt Jemima to collect whelks, which she was forced to eat when they got home – she has never touched shellfish since.

Apparently when I was a baby in my pram I was left outside my grandmother's house – it was safe to do things like that back then – but someone in a flat at the top of the tenement threw a tin can out of the window. The can had been opened with the old fashioned jagged-edged can opener, and when it hit me, it stuck into the top of my head. I was told that if it had been a quarter of an inch further over, I would not be sitting typing this. My first encounter the Scottish Health Service!

I have two sisters and one brother and one of my first

memories was of my brother holding me up to the window of our top flat to show me the searchlights zooming across the sky. I did not know what the celebrations were, as it was 1947, but I remember being terrified. I always seemed to be terrified of something or other when I was a child, and some things I shall explain later.

I can remember the flat quite well even though I left it when I was only five years old. The 'close' is the entrance hall from which there are two or three flats leading off each landing, and on the half-landing there was a toilet for the two or three families to use. At the back end of the close was a long passage which housed the toilet for the families of the ground floor to use. The problem with this was that when you had to take the rubbish out to the 'midden' you had to pass this very gloomy passage to get to the back court. Fortunately I was too small to have to do this too often. The lighting on the landing was very dim as it was lit by a gas lamp which always seemed to pop when I was walking up the stairs. It made eerie shadows on the walls, so every time I walked up the stairs to the top flat (why couldn't we live on the ground floor?) I sang as loudly as I could – what good that would do I had no idea, but sing I did.

It's been brought to my mind recently that there was a real panic when the toilet on the landing below ours became blocked and the families living there had to come and use ours; and that meant at least fifty people were using the same loo. Fortunately my Mum was particularly fastidious and was pouring down what was then the equivalent of bleach every five minutes. I can only imagine Mum standing against the toilet door, giving everyone only five minutes each; it's a wonder that there wasn't a clocking-on machine installed.

The flat had one bedroom and a kitchen. There were six of us. Until I was five, I slept with my Mum and Dad in a bed recessed in the kitchen wall. I vaguely remember being crushed against the wall many times and so I grew up being claustrophobic – and I still am. My two sisters slept in the bedroom with a curtain separating them from my brother. My older sister Jenny recalls the time when she was plaiting the fringes of the bedspread and one of the fringes was particularly cold; looking closer, she found that she was making a very pretty plait that included a dead mouse's tail. I supposed she screamed but she didn't tell me that; I'm sure I would have done.

The kitchen-cum-dining room-cum bedroom was small, but I remember quite vividly the radio, which looked as if it had a smiley face when it was switched on. I also recall my father singing along with all the songs on the Light Programme, with me on his knee, listening to Bernard Braden (was it all that time ago?) So my childhood was filled with songs of old and I grew up knowing all the words of songs by Al Johnson, Bing Crosby and some names I can't quite remember. At the sink there was a brass tap that was polished very regularly; if my memory serves me well it looked like the handle of a walking stick and for some reason it could be brought down towards the sink, maybe to polish?

We had no washing facilities other than the 'steamy', a public wash house. Going to the steamy was also a social occasion as the ladies had a chance to catch up on gossip and to swap stories over the huge stone sinks. Mum took me there several times and I remember the noise of running water, spinners, driers and constant talk. The washing was then put in huge driers, called horses, which were particularly useful contraptions as there was no place to dry the clothes at home. After the washing was done it was neatly folded and put in a big pram, hopefully vacated by the baby, and pushed home. There was a small rope and pole contraption which hung out of the window and on a sunny day the 'smalls' were hung out.

I also recall the white sandshoes (or gym shoes) drying out on the window ledge after being whitened by a tube of something which dried to a sort of chalky effect. Whatever would anyone have thought if they had received a smack on the head from a flying gym shoe, blown off the ledge by a gust of wind?

We had no proper oven in the flat so there were no cakes or buns made, but I was told that the person living in the flat before us, a plumber, made a device from copper tubing with holes in it and connected it to the gas pipe. It would be a brave soul that would try to bake a cake in those circumstances, but try they did. Jenny baked fairy cakes for the first time and she was most upset when they were all eaten, because she wanted to look at them for just a while longer before they were devoured. I have a great aversion to tea leaves, as I vividly recall that when not enough cups were available for tea, someone had to drink from a jam jar. I think that was possibly me, as I can still see the tea leaves swirling around the glass when the sugar was stirred in. Even to this day when my friend Sheila and I go for a coffee every Tuesday, she always teases me about the amount of coffee left in my cup when we've finished, as I don't want to swallow tea leaves, even in coffee.

There was no toilet in the flat, so to me it was always such a frightening event to have to go the loo, especially in the middle of the night. My parents, especially my father, were very Victorian in their outlook and we were not allowed to mention bodily functions, so when I was very small I remember having to sit on the potty behind the table and being terribly embarrassed even at that age. Growing up was no better: Dad would nod to my Mum to let my sisters know if their underskirts or straps were showing and he would say to Mum something like, "Tell them about that". He wouldn't know what to say himself.

We had to share our flat with other occupants of the four-footed variety. I was told that when I was very small, I was pointing to the dog and muttering "Doggy eat!" in my best two-year-old language. What I was pointing to was a great big rat tucking into the dog's dinner. I clearly remember the time when George was at one end of the brass fender and Mum was at the other, one armed with a brush the other with a shovel, trying to coax out a mouse with some delicacy, but neither was quick enough to catch the little blighter. Ellen remembers someone called 'Sandshoe Harry' who crept around in his gym shoes, hence the name, and who would inject the victim with some unspeakable concoction, rending them unconscious. When she told me about this I really do think that he was a figment of many a mother's imagination to keep the unfortunate child a bit better behaved.

My mum and dad got married when she was seventeen and he twenty. I think they had to get married, something that was completely frowned on in those days, so different now. They lived with my granddad when they were first married and things were not easy for them. My mum was a very hard worker. During the war, she worked in a rope-making factory even although she was only five feet tall. She told me what was involved in rope making, saying that she had to gather up great wads of hemp and flick it up and down with great force. She also recalled that several of the women working there had some terrible accidents, one poor soul was scalped when her hair was caught in the twisting rope.

Mum and Dad moved in with Granddad, as he was on his own after his wife had died a few years earlier. Mum kept the house spotless and she had electricity installed, so their little home was cosy and comfortable. Things were quite strained after my brother was born, as Granddad probably did not appreciate a new infant in his house. My parents moved out and shortly afterwards he took in lodgers, who did not appreciate his drinking and promptly threw him out. So they ended up with the house which Mum worked so hard to make a home and my mum and dad ended up in the tenement I later grew up in.

I didn't know my grandfather very well but learned much later that he had been in the First World War and was never the same when he came home. I always remember him being drunk but I had no clue why he drank so much; probably like many millions of men he was trying to forget the horrors of seeing their compatriots being slaughtered and mutilated. It's a shame that it's only when you are older and learn more of the world can you understand the atrocities and why the men wanted to obliterate any memories of the Great War.

A good memory of my grandfather was when I came home from a tap dancing class and he was visiting Mum and Dad, and he asked me to dance. A blackboard appeared from somewhere and was put on the floor and I had to 'show off' which, being a timid little thing, was very hard. I loved his moustache that sort of drooped over his mouth. You could hardly see his lips as it sort of jumped up and down every time he spoke.

My father was a coppersmith, a vocation which probably no one has ever heard of nowadays. He was put into an apprenticeship by his father and he hated every day he was there. I found out many years later that he wanted to be a journalist, a job he would have been so good at as he was a very well read man. But who had ever heard of a journalist coming from a working class family from Govan? His head teacher wrote in his report book that he thought my father would go far.

Dad suffered from dermatitis, which meant that he could not always work, so my mum went out to work as a cleaner. She worked in some of the grander houses in Glasgow and there she found out how other half lived. Some of the ladies that she cleaned for were very generous and gave her clothes and sometimes food that was surplus. Other people tended to look rather scathingly at the cleaner and would walk around her without acknowledgement. She remembers one incident when one of these superior ladies gave her a pair of her husband's shoes and when she got home, there were enormous holes in the soles. There was a good fire in the grate that night.

We all went to Sunday school, as I think most children of that era did. My sisters remember more about this than I do but they always spoke well of their Sunday school teachers and they exchanged Christmas cards until the dear old ladies died. I remember one Christmas time when they had a projector to show a Charlie Chaplin film but thinking that the best part of the evening was when they had to run the film backwards to rewind. What a treat to see the little man running in reverse with his feet sticking out.

An annual event that we always looked forward to

was the Sunday School trip. This was a great occasion, when a horse and cart pulled up and all the children would scramble up on the cart and off they went. No 'health and safety' then, thank goodness. I suppose they must have thought they were going to the other side of Scotland because it took a long time to get where they going but I think it was actually only a mile or two. They were all given a little parcel containing a sandwich and a biscuit and I suppose these were all eaten before they left the street. As a sort of cultural visit (I don't think that phrase was around at that time) we were taken to David Livingstone's house in Blantyre and I still remember thinking, even at that age, why he would wear a collar and tie in all that heat.

I always believed in God and the stories I heard in the Bible; there was no way that these could not be true. The only thing I found difficult to understand was how God could listen to the prayers of every boy and girl if they all went to bed at the same time each night. I believed in God as a large grandfather figure sitting on a cloud in Heaven, who had a long white beard and who wouldn't really have much time for me. But there was always a lovely feeling of being somewhere special in Sunday school. The teachers had lovely speaking voices, so different from the broad accents I normally heard. Mum and Dad never went to church, as far as I remember, but I recall Dad saying that he thought that Jesus would have been a Socialist or Communist as He wanted everyone in the world to have equal shares in all things. I really didn't understand any of this at the time.

There was always something going on in the Sunday school hall and I went there for tap dancing lessons. I was so proud of my white tap shoes which made a lovely clicking noise as I walked down the eight flights of stairs in the hall. I always have loved dancing. We learned many catchy little tunes and we went home singing things like 'I am a fine musician, I practise every day on the piccolo', and so on.

My sister Ellen got a job in the Co-op and when I went in to the shop with Mum I was fascinated by the overhead cables with little boxes flying around, carrying the bills and cash.

Jenny had a job in a tobacco factory and I remember the funny smell from her overalls when she came home. She was obviously very unhappy in her job and one of the lovely Sunday School teachers told her that she would pay for Jenny to go to college to train as a Comptometer operator. I think that was the best thing that could have happened to her and Jenny was always so grateful for the opportunity that she was given.

My mum and dad had a turbulent relationship. I think she felt cheated that her life was so lacking in affection and love. Sometimes I think that men of that era, and maybe in particular Scottish men, found it difficult or less than manly to show any affection to their wives and children. Money was always short and my memories were of quarrels, because my father always sought solace in the pub. He was a very sociable chap and was happiest when he was singing with his peers in his working men's club. He was a wonderful singer and went for several auditions but unfortunately was never given the opportunity to have a singing career. Apparently he was once told that he didn't have the 'right look'! I think he was gutted by that, as another dream bit the dust.

Most Friday nights held some surprises when Dad came home with a parcel tucked under his jacket, and we looked forward to finding out what he had acquired from the pub. Huge bars of chocolate were produced from a rolled up newspaper. It was cooking chocolate and sort of claggy and stuck to the roof of your mouth, but not knowing real chocolate, we ate it with great relish. One time he produced an extra-large parcel from his jacket and slapped a huge fish on the table, to which Mum announced that she didn't have a big enough frying pan!

My mum had a friend that she had known since childhood; a lady so different in nature to my mum that we all wondered how they could have remained friends for so many years. She called a spade a 'blankety blank shovel', etc. Mum told us that when her friend used words that we had never heard in our house, we would laugh, probably from embarrassment. Although my dad worked in a place akin to the shipyards, I never heard him swear once in his eighty six years. He always said that you didn't have enough vocabulary if you had to use foul language.

I recall a time when I cried so much when Mum and her friend went out one evening, much to the annoyance of my sisters who had to look after me. We joke about it now but Jenny has told me that before being put to bed she would wash my face with a dry face cloth. I have always said that it was all her fault that I was not beautiful.

Mum had another friend, Nell, who introduced her to a couple of ladies who came from a very up-market part of Glasgow. They both visited them every Wednesday. I never found out what the relationship was but we knew that every Thursday morning, there would be a big box of cakes, the like of which we had only seen in shop windows; it was wonderful.

The late Forties and Fifties were a time when children

could play out for hours and hours without any worry from the family. It was innocent fun, playing marbles and shops – using pieces of glass as money. If you could find a piece of glass with gold on it, you could buy up the shop. We played in mud, which in Glasgow is called 'glabber', forming it into shapes then jumping up and down on it. We were sent out to play in our tattiest clothes, as our school clothes were precious.

Everyone in the tenements around us was just as poor as we were, although I didn't know I was poor. A memory, which always makes me cringe, was the day a photographer came to where all the children were playing and took pictures of us all. We all had our dirtiest clothes on for playing and hadn't a care in the world, so we complied when he told us to stand against the wall and smile, but this little episode was to cost Mum two shillings and six pence. I'm afraid it didn't go down too well, for when the photograph came back I looked like an unwashed waif. I was presented with the photo after I got married – what a sight.

The family across the landing was much better off than we were. I had never seen a fur coat except on our neighbour. It was made of beaver lamb and I recall standing next to her, surreptitiously rubbing my hands on this fantastic material, thinking it was wonderful and soft. I was so glad she didn't catch me because there was another frightening side to this 'lady', as I told my mum several years ago.

My mum often asked her to look after me when she went out working and she would let me help her wash the dishes. She had a pair of rubber gloves which she used to wash up with, something I had never seen before but when I was sitting in the chair afterwards she would creep up on me with the rubber gloves, which she had blown up, and would wave them so close to my face that I was petrified. She chased me all over the house with this and I recall sobbing uncontrollably and hiding down the side of her bed. My mum was incandescent with rage when, years later, I told her of this.

One more thing this charming lady did was that she told me that if I did anything wrong or told tales, the man in the moon would get me. When I look back, it seems ludicrous that I would be so scared, but being brought up to believe that all 'older people' were right, I was just plain terrified. To this day, I cannot look at a full moon without a shiver of a bad memory creeping over me.

Jenny and Ellen had more to do with this lady as they were slightly older and were friendly with her daughter. They told me that when they had something new to wear, especially on May Day, the woman would lift up their skirts and pretend to blow her nose on them; a most unpleasant trick. When her daughter had a birthday party, another thing that was a novelty, she told my sisters not to bring any hankies or socks, as she had more than enough.

My mum told me that one day when the neighbour was looking after me, I went home, across the landing, and told her that Mrs Reid had 'took' coal and a carrot from our house. I think maybe she was getting her own back and I was very afraid to go back into her house.

Another thing about our neighbour was that her husband had a very good job and could afford anything they wanted, but apparently she used to 'borrow' a piece of cheese from the other neighbour on the landing. This lady had eleven children and was so poor that she could hardly afford to give anything away. The door on their flat had been kicked in so many times that a blanket hung in its place. The man of the household, a known womaniser, was a tic-tac man at the racecourse and was always dressed immaculately in a Crombie-style coat and little trilby hat. His poor family had literally nothing. The girls had no socks, vests, sometimes even no knickers, and I can't even imagine that they had enough to eat. I left that area before learning what happened to them but I think my sisters would probably have kept in touch. My Mum really liked the neighbour and I think she felt really sorry for her, as they were obviously far worse off than we were.

A great day would be when the Gas Man called to empty the meter. As he counted the money in the box, he would stack the pennies in little piles. I don't know how the arrangement went, but he would always give back a neat little pile of coins to Mum, who would smile and put them away. I think it must have happened at every house he visited and then the local shops would be visited.

When I was sent to the shops it would be to the Co-op, where after my purchases I had to remember my mum's dividend number, which I remember to this day, 'eleven five eight five'. Mum would always want the receipts so she could keep an eye on what she was due. She would count up the receipts and with each additional purchase would add it to the list and then calculate what was owed.

My brother George was very protective of my sisters and disapproved of any make-up that they would try to wear. "Are your lips bleeding?" he would say to them, "Go and wash it off!" When Jenny was eighteen, Ellen bought her a lipstick that she hoped to put on after she went out of the house. But alas! I found it and tried to do what the ladies did, smearing it all over my face, before smartly twisting it back into the tube to complete the job. I looked like a smiley Joker from Batman.

Recently Mum told me about a couple who lived in the bottom flat of our tenement. The woman was a genteel lady who had obviously been brought up in a different world from any of the other neighbours. She spoke beautifully and held herself so well. Her husband was totally different, an ordinary working man. When they first arrived she was the talk of the 'close' as the people saw what beautiful linen and fine tablecloths she had. I don't know how, but soon afterwards they seemed to sink into a decline. Things became really bad financially for them, even more so than the rest of the neighbours, so much so that they had to burn the furniture for heating. When that was all gone they burned the lino.

When Mrs. Kelly died, one of their youngest children died and funeral expenses were out of the question, so a little homemade box was used. It was the saddest sight anyone had ever seen when Mr Kelly walked down the road carrying the little coffin. When told of this, I thought Catherine Cookson would have made a wonderful family saga from their terribly sad story, although I'm sure she would have written a happy ending.

When my sister Jenny was young, she had hair that looked as if it had streaks in it, something you would pay a fortune for today. A teacher in her school believed that Jenny had used dye on her hair and Jenny was taken every day for weeks to have her hair washed to get rid of the 'dye'. I'm sure that her red scalp would have caused more irritation than a few natural steaks.

Ellen told me of an incident when she was delivering papers. A lorry passed by and some potatoes fell off; she grabbed them and ran home as fast as she could, threw the potatoes in the door, breathing heavily, but I'm sure feeling pretty pleased with herself with her 'spoils'. I think she believed that the 'Polis' were after her.

Mum would make butter in a milk bottle – the old fashioned bottle with a wide neck. She took the cream off the top every morning and when she had enough, she shook the bottle vigorously until the butter would eventually emerge. I don't think she ever suffered from repetitive strain injury but it wouldn't have surprised me if she had.

Apart from my childish fears, there are also good memories, mostly to do with music. My father was a great singer and he would make up little songs to the popular tunes of the day. He would have us sitting round the table while he tapped out the rhythm of a song with a spoon and we would try to guess the song. He also would baffle us with riddles, for instance the old chestnut, 'Sisters and brothers have I none, but that man's father is my father's son'. It took us a long time before he would tell us the answer. Another was, 'If Moses was the son of Pharaoh's daughter, he was also the daughter of Pharaoh's son'. We always said, "Dad, how could Moses be a daughter?" His answer would always the same: it depends where the apostrophe is placed!

Music has and always will be a great part of my life, but I didn't know to what extent it would help me through future traumas. Even to this day I can remember an enormous number of songs that must have been burned into my brain and they have come in very handy.

The infant school I went to was only a few hundred yards from home. I enjoyed lessons and was fairly clever, especially at English and spelling etc. I recall the first day at school when I was given a small board with sand on it and we had to copy what the teacher wrote on the blackboard. I was told to copy the number five, which the teacher drew as a postman with a big fat tummy and a hat. I can only remember 'postman number five'; goodness knows what the other numbers were called.

My childhood education went by without much happening. At home we were never given any encouragement for our schooling, although we were always encouraged to read. I can clearly remember being very excited about getting ninety seven percent in an exam, but my excitement was short- lived when my father asked what happened to the other three. Maybe he thought that it would encourage me to do better, but it only made me feel very inadequate, a disposition that lasted for an extremely long time. My sister Ellen always had her nose in a book and I followed her example. I recall being given a copy of 'Gulliver's Travels' and I read it so often that I could recite verbatim the first ten pages.

When I was about four, I had to have my tonsils out. I remember being told by the nurse that when I woke up I would have some ice cream to cool my throat down. I felt cheated because all I remember was having a glass of a drink that looked as if it had two layers on it. At the top it was clear and the bottom was orange and I later found out that it was castor oil mixed with orange juice and of course it didn't mix – it was horrible. I was so disappointed that I never got any ice cream. A few days after coming home, I suddenly started to bring up blood and was immediately taken to hospital the middle of the night. Having no transport, I was carried in turn by Mum, Dad and George. On being seen in the A&E department I was told that it was just the after-effects of the tonsil operation. As I was being seen to, I heard a bit of a commotion going on in the corridor and I found out later that George had fainted and was having more treatment than I was.

When Mum and Dad knew that they were eventually to be re-housed, Mum started to save up for some new furniture. We couldn't wait to see the purchases. She was the proud owner of two smokers' chairs, which was really strange as not one of the family smoked! They were just two armchairs that were fitted with two ash trays at either side of the arms and two places down the side for papers or magazines. She also bought a roll of lino ready to be put down on the floor of our new house. These new treasures sat in a corner of the room for two years until they were ready to be installed in the new house. Of course, at the time we didn't know how long we would be waiting for the move.

When the tenement we lived in was declared too dangerous we were housed in another tenement. This time there were three bedrooms, a living room, kitchen and, the best part of all, a bathroom. It had a long lobby and the lino was immediately put down and it looked just grand. The day we moved in, a friend of Mum's was helping with the fitting and a well-deserved cup of tea was made but unfortunately there was no spoon, so the new door key was used and we drank the first beverage in our new kitchen.

I remember that the walls in every room had a white powdery coating on them, which I recall Mum called distemper (and later I found out that's also what dogs sometimes get). In the sitting room the previous tenant must have had infinite patience, dabbing a sponge with a different coloured blob of paint every few inches. When the time came to wallpaper each room, I was the one who had to wipe over the paste table. I think this must have been the worst job because the cloth got incredibly sticky after every wipe. When the 'border' had to be bought, I was sent to the shop with a sample and I was fascinated to see the lady put the paper through a machine to trim the edges.

Each Sunday we all had chores to do. On the radio every Sunday was 'Two Way Family Favourites' and I clearly recall putting dusters on my feet and sliding up and down the lobby to the wonderful music. There was every type of music from Classical to the modern-day 'crooners', so I learned to keep time to Ravel's 'Bolero' and Perry Como's 'Catch A Falling Star', skating up and down with not a care in the world. I also had to clean the brass candlesticks and a brass plaque with a ship in full sail on it; Brasso makes your fingernails really black.

Of course I had to change schools, which as a timid little thing was quite an ordeal, but I enjoyed it thoroughly and did quite well. Another hospital scenario comes to mind, when at three o'clock one afternoon I was coming out of the classroom. A lad from another class was running along the corridor, swinging a wooden briefcase, which apparently his father had made, and it landed right on the bridge of my nose. Fortunately nothing was broken, not even the case, but I had two enormous black eyes and the bruising went right down under my chin and lasted for many weeks. There is always an upside to things that happen to you, and every time I went out with my Mum or sisters, everybody I met said the usual "Oh dear what happened?" and they gave me money, probably feeling sorry for me. I remember thinking, how can I keep this effect on my face to make a little more money?

I enjoyed singing in the school choir and even joined

them in some competitions at the St Andrews Hall, a superb building. I always wanted to be in the back row, hiding behind a taller girl. I don't think that I really took in the whole experience and I don't remember enjoying it, but I would love to go back and relive it, if only that were possible.

Mum and Dad were wonderful dancers and would often go out with their friends to the local working men's club. We all grew up being reasonably good dancers and still enjoy a good 'Dashing White Sergeant' if we can find enough people to join in!

When they were a bit better off, she would go up to town to buy a lovely 'frock'. She would often take me with her and sometimes I would see something that I thought would suit her; even although I was still only very young I seemed to have an eye for nice clothes.

When my mum was thirty seven she had to have a hysterectomy and her appendix removed at the same time, and she was in hospital for a long time, as you were back then. She wasn't at all well and when she came home it was ages before she could do even the lightest of housework. I came home from school one day to find her crying in the kitchen. There had been a terrific storm and she couldn't close the kitchen window. The rain was pouring in through the window and she didn't have the strength to close it.

My father's work ran a scheme where any relative of the employee could go to a convalescent home, so when her health improved, Mum and I went to a beautiful big house right next to the sea. My first recollection was the luxury of the soft beds and all the matching curtains and bedspreads, the huge bathroom and the wonderful view from the bedroom. Since I was the only child there, I was allowed to ring the gong for breakfast, lunch and dinner, and I felt very important. The only problem was that we were sharing a room with another lady who snored so incredibly loudly that Mum and I just cried all night. We felt so bad that we had to report it to the Matron and she seemed not to have had complaints before about this lady. Fortunately we were moved to a two-bedded room but we always felt very uncomfortable when we met her. Apart from that, we had a wonderful time and Mum felt much better when we went home.

During the 'holiday' we would go into the nearest town on the bus. I had my first taste of coffee in a café and I loved it. I think it was Camp Coffee and it was made with hot milk but it was the best hot drink I had ever had – and no tea leaves. Very occasionally, I treat myself to a bottle of Camp Coffee and wallow in lovely memories.

I had plenty of friends and in summer we spent all our play time in the park opposite our house. Glasgow has some beautiful parks and I suppose like every other child in Glasgow we thought they were wonderful to play in, using our imaginations for all kinds of games until it was time to go home, mucky and exhausted. When going out to play we took a bottle of water and a biscuit or something that Mum had given us, so we could stay out for a little longer. When we were playing round the back courts and felt a little peckish, we would shout up to our respective windows, "Ma can you throw me over a 'piece 'n jam'?", which translates as a jam sandwich. If you were lucky and the respective mum was in a good mood, the 'piece' would come flying out of the window, hopefully wrapped in some newspaper; if not you had to be a darn good catcher.

We went swimming in the public baths, which were fortunately quite close to us and I quickly learned to swim.

Ellen told me that once she was wearing a new woollen swimming costume and on coming up from the water, she discovered that the costume was suddenly extremely heavy and long, and she had to make several adjustments to her 'dress' as she walked up each step from the pool. Whoever thought that wool would make a suitable swimming costume? The swimming baths seemed huge and noisy, with changing cubicles all around the sides of the baths, so that you could keep an eye on your clothes. On the way back home, exhausted and full of fun, we would call into the chip shop for some sustenance to get us back home. Then we would repeat it all again the next week.

Mum always went back to the shops where we used to live so that she could meet her old neighbours. I was dragged along and I got to know every shop keeper in our old haunts. I well remember that when she wanted something new, she would work and wait to get the money. But on one occasion she saw in the window of a little shop that sold everything, the most beautiful bone china tea set; white with tiny little black dots and a gold rim. She looked so longingly and so long in the window and then ran in and bought it 'on tick'. When it was paid off, she brought it home and immediately put it in a cupboard; and to this day, none of the family has ever had a cup of tea from it.

I also remember one day when Mum bought a beautiful piece of meat from her local butcher. It was something special for tea and I said to her, "That tastes like nectar" (I know it should have been Ambrosia). She seemed quite annoyed and replied "I shall complain to Bob the butcher in the morning". I also recall the fish shops Mum would visit and especially the ladies with very red hands, covered in fish scales, the clogs they wore and the ice they used to throw over the fish in the window.

So my younger years were really straightforward and happy. There was always music in our house and my sisters and I would lie in bed on a Sunday morning singing. We would harmonise and thoroughly enjoy ourselves. They sang songs from Sunday school and from the popular songs of that era, Frank Sinatra, Perry Como, etc., so I grew up with a variety of music going round in my head. My siblings decided that between them they would buy a Radiogram and we waited with bated breath for the arrival of this wonderful addition to the house.

The only problem I remember was the clash of musical tastes, my sisters wanted the pop songs of the day but my brother's taste was more on the classical lines. I think they waited till each went out and then sneaked a quick play of their favourite record, a sort of rota system or shift arrangement. When my brother George was in the Army he brought back from foreign parts a lot of LPs of musicals that we had never heard of: 'South Pacific', 'The King and I', 'Oklahoma' and 'Carousel'. We listened to them over and over again and I could recite every word by the time I was eleven. I was also bewitched by a very famous Frank Sinatra LP called 'Songs for Swinging Lovers', which I could recite verbatim before I was eleven, even being aware of his very special voice and the wonderful arrangement on each track.

Chapter 2

The year 1958 was particularly traumatic for all the family. There were two births, both my sisters having babies and both were traumatic events for them. I had been at my secondary school for only five days, wearing my brand new uniform, including a blazer with yellow trim and school badge along with skirt and leather briefcase, all of which had cost my parents a lot of money.

On 2nd October that year (my dad's birthday), my friend Betty and I were walking home from school, going a different way than usual. We stopped to say goodbye and the next thing I knew I woke up, lying on the ground with lots of people staring down at me. I couldn't quite understand what was happening and then I saw my sister bending down telling me that everything would be alright.

I don't remember much after that except that there was something wrong with my left arm. Lying in the hospital emergency room, I vividly remember the nurse cutting off my brand new blazer and me saying to her that Mum would be furious with her if she saw what was she was doing to my new school uniform. Mum had been coming back from work and she heard the ambulance rushing up the street where I had been knocked down. She told me many years later that she always said that when an ambulance passed by, she hoped that it would be nobody she knew!

When I awoke the next morning I was told that a lorry

had been towing another and the tow rope had snapped and the second lorry went out of control. It mounted the pavement and crashed into the telephone kiosk that Betty and I were standing next to, and apparently the broken glass severed my arm. The matron stood over me and told me, in a very matter-of-fact voice with no sign of sympathy, that my arm had been severed in an accident. I couldn't understand it because I could feel that my arm was still there. Then a lady from the Salvation Army came and prayed with me, telling me exactly the same as the matron. It was all still a dream to me and remained so for a few days until I could sit up and look down the bed to see if what they had told me was true. It was.

My friend Betty was in the next bed to me. She had suffered a broken pelvis and was in a sort of sling contraption, so between us we were a pretty pair. Betty took a long time to heal and was in hospital for several months. I remember going to visit her at Christmas and there she was, still lying there. I felt a bit guilty that I could walk away and she could not. We saw each other several times after she came out of hospital but for some reason we drifted apart, which I often regretted. It would have been nice to exchange scar stories.

I was inundated with cards, flowers and gifts from people I didn't even know. They had read about it in the newspaper. When I left hospital after three weeks I took home twenty five pounds of chocolates, that was after giving some of them to the wonderful medical staff. Everyone in the hospital was extremely kind and helpful. There was a lovely nurse called Nurse Leon, who came from the West Indies and it was her job to look after me, and she did. A lady I didn't really know came to visit me and she brought me the most beautiful flowers. Mum never had spare money to spend on flowers, so this was a treat. They were huge-headed chrysanthemums in a bronze colour; I had never seen anything like them before. They lasted as long I was in hospital and I don't think I've ever seen the like of them again.

I was in hospital for just over three weeks. At that age I didn't know what was meant by a safe haven, but although I was desperate to go home I was also afraid of the whole new world that would open up to me as soon as I left hospital. It wasn't until I left hospital that I was aware that Jenny had not come to visit me and when I was old enough to understand, I learned that she was advised not to see me, as she was having such a bad time in her pregnancy that the shock might not have been good for her.

I was brought home by taxi and I had a strange feeling of being in a dream and that this was happening to someone else. I didn't want to go to bed that first night home despite being so tired and I had to be persuaded, but then everyone kept tiptoeing in and out of my room just to check how I was doing. I could hear them whispering and Mum crying – and it was me that was causing all the fuss. I really don't remember if I was in much pain but I do recall that I couldn't touch my stump as it gave me a sort of electric shock so I tried not to do this, even although sometimes it itched but there was nothing to scratch, which was quite disconcerting and it took me many years before I got used to it.

I had to have a district nurse in every other day to change the dressing. Mum would stay with me when this was being done and I always asked her not to look at my arm. I don't know why, maybe this was my way of not really believing what had happened, for if Mum didn't see it,

31

maybe it wasn't true. Getting used to eating with just a fork was my first test, which I passed, and I found that I could cope with most of the other day-to-day trials. People around us were also very good to me and my school friends came to visit many times.

I was having trouble with my shoulder and I found I couldn't really relax, so Mum took me to a physiotherapist. She made me lie under a heat lamp for thirty minutes and just as I was dropping off she would come in and massage my shoulders and back, it was heavenly. I went there every week for quite a long time but as soon as each session was finished I was just as tense as before.

I went back to school about four months later, during which time all my class mates had been taught algebra and some complicated maths. Well, I thought it was complicated because I had missed the early teaching and I could never catch up. I'm sure the teachers were trying their best to help me but they might as well have been speaking in Norwegian for all I understood. This was the start of my great lack of confidence and a huge inferiority complex. On returning to school I felt that everyone I had known before had a different attitude towards me and I knew they were all talking about me.

The things I enjoyed most in school were English and Music. My English teacher was wonderful, although Jenny couldn't understand why, because she had been her teacher at the High School and had not been very pleasant. But she taught us all about Greek Mythology, which I loved and my imagination could run riot. My music teacher was very good but she would occasionally ask me to sing on my own, which I hated as it drew attention to me. She did this regularly, perhaps hoping it would help me by showing me how wonderful music could soothe and heal a troubled youngster.

Not having the confidence to tell the Maths teachers that I didn't understand what they were saying, and at that time no-one voluntarily spoke to the teachers, I just had to struggle on, and of course, what little confidence I had soon vanished into thin air. I was totally overwhelmed by everything. When I looked in the mirror all I saw was a twelve-year-old misfit. I had never heard of that saying before, but it applied. Everybody was very sympathetic and kind, but my poor mum didn't know how to treat me. She wrapped me up in cotton wool which was only natural, and I would have done the same for my children. When we met her friends, she would stand behind me and mouth words to them, saying things like "She's not well" (the way Les Dawson used to do). I don't think she realised that I was aware of everything she said.

George was one of the last conscripts in the Army and when he came home from Cyprus he told Mum – without my knowledge of course – that I should be left to work out for myself how I was going to do everything I needed to do. Jenny's husband George was also trying to get Mum and Dad to let me figure things out for myself, but I went through every day in a kind of dream, doing things by rote and not really taking things in, but trying to keep 'normal'.

My sister Jenny's sister-in-law ran a swimming club and I was taken along, hoping that there weren't too many people who would stare at me. I was surprised to discover that I could still swim and did not go round in circles! I got to know everyone quite well, so I didn't feel out of place and got to enjoy it really well. One incident I remember was that the swimming club organized a day trip to the seaside and all the family went. On arriving at our destination it was rather breezy and, despite the sun, we sat there all day freezing. When it was time to go home, George and Rena came walking round the other side from where we all were and they were burned to a crisp; the sun had been scorching just two hundred yards from where we sat huddled together in our coats, drinking soup from a flask.

I had to be fitted with an artificial arm; the posh name now is a prosthetic. It was agony at first. The traps, or harness, was attached to the shoulder of the prosthetic, went under my right arm and right round my back. Although the kind people at the Limb Fitting Centre did their best, it was agony for a long time until I got used to it. It certainly helped with certain things I had to do; for example, at school we were doing shorthand typing and I could take the hand off my artificial arm and insert a steel finger with a rubber end, which I used for typing and became very good at it. I was also allowed to look at the keyboard, when the other girls weren't. My mum and dad bought me a portable typewriter and I used to practice for hours, and at the end of the second year at school I won first prize for Shorthand and Typing.

During this time I was suffering a lot of minor illnesses. I had the worst case of chickenpox the doctor had ever seen. I scratched one of the spots on my face and it left a scar – another reason to feel inadequate. This sounds really pathetic, but I did not realise that I was having a nervous breakdown, as they used to call it; depression or post-traumatic stress, as it's called now. I was also still feeling all of my missing arm and couldn't understand why, time after time, I would be doubled up in agony with the most awful pains in my 'phantom' hand. There was nothing I could about it because it was all in my brain. My hand also itched sometimes, which was quite annoying, and to this day I still have pins and needles in the palm of my hand. Strange what the brain can do to you.

Jenny and George had married and moved into a flat in the next close to ours, with George's dad. His mum had died a few years earlier. Jenny had a neighbour in the flat below who seemed to want to take her under her wing. When Jenny was hanging out her washing she would hear a knock at the window and the neighbour would tell her not to hang the towels next to the shirts, to put the tea towels next and then the smaller items. I'm sure Jenny tried to hang her washing out before prying eyes were up and about. The problem with living in a tenement is that you could only hang out your washing in the back court once a week and there was a rota system for the eight families sharing the space. Mum also thought it was handy having Jenny living so near and I was often sent on a Sunday to borrow something that was lacking in our own kitchen.

Back to the nervous breakdown. It started one day when I was walking to school and I caught sight of myself in a shop window. I could not believe that it was me – maybe it wasn't – so my mind told me. I was soon frightened to look in any mirror because that same sensation came over me. I couldn't explain it to anyone and we were not a family for sharing our feelings, so I tried to get through the days as best I could. In those days there were no counsellors and I was told to get over it, or to "go out and do something". That's the one thing I wanted to do but I couldn't.

I used to wake up in the morning and for a split second everything was normal until the black cloud slowly returned to sit on my shoulder and a concrete slab pressed on my chest. I wasn't aware that what I was going through was 'normal' and without anyone to talk to, how could I know that it would get much worse? How could I know that it would eventually get better in time? It seems unfair of me to say that I had no one to talk to, but we did not share our feelings and so I went through my trials alone. I used to dream that I could do everything that the other girls could do. It was the time of the beehive hair styles and I couldn't back-comb my hair; so, again I felt different, plain and ugly. My ambition was to be beautiful, but how could that be possible? Now that I am much older I think that being beautiful must have its drawbacks, or so I keep telling myself.

As a family, we went on holiday to Leven on the east coast of Scotland. We went to the same place every year, as most people did back then. One incident that is etched indelibly on my mind is the time that my mum bought a new suitcase. When she brought it home we were told that it was an expandable one and could hold everyone's clothes. "Fantastic!" we declared, until poor Dad had to lift the blooming thing. On arrival at Leven we were approached by a young man asking if he could help us with the case for a shilling; Dad said "No thank you". Was he sorry! We were staying at least two miles from the station and his arms ended up looking like Guy the Gorilla!

We were staying with a lady called Mrs Thompson, who had a lovely Italian accent, and we found out that she had married a soldier she met in Italy. She took a bit of a shine to me and would cook us some lovely meals. Some we had never tried before – she dipped cauliflower in egg and then fried it; it was delicious. Not everything was perfect: she would wash my hair with Omo soap powder. Fortunately my hair didn't fall out but I was always wary when it rained in case I had a halo of bubbles round my head or a rainbow round my shoulders.

I always tried to buy a little something for Mum and Dad when we were on holiday and I'll never forget a little ornament that I gave them which was hung up by the window. It was a figure 'Indian Joe', wearing a little apron on which was written, 'Apron blue – sky is too, Apron pink – weather stink'. It seemed to work, although I've no idea why, but it always made us smile.

When on holiday we would go to a fairground that was there all summer. Not being one for going on rides and things, I tried my hand at the shooting gallery. I had to bend my artificial arm, lean it on the counter and rest the air rifle on the hand. It was rock steady and I shot very well, winning every time, much to the annoyance of the stall holder. We almost had to buy another suitcase to bring back all of my 'winnings', which included twenty four little glasses, a fire screen, a vase and various other useless things.

One year when we went on holiday, Jenny and George and Alison, their daughter, were staying in another house and I was asked to stay overnight with them. The house was huge, very old and dark, and had gas lighting, like something out of a horror movie – but I bet a property developer would give his eye teeth for it now. My room was on the second floor and when I went to bed I was convinced that I was going to die if I fell asleep; even the thought of going to bed was an ordeal. I was absolutely petrified and it was a long time before I could get rid of that fear. It was another symptom of depression. It was such a terrible time for me that even now I can remember so clearly how terrified I was.

A little aside: Mum was and still is very superstitious, and she was distraught over an incident with a gift I received from my sister Ellen. It was a lovely gold signet ring with

37

my initials on it, and as my maiden name was Mitchell and my middle name is Reid, the initials were 'ARM'. Another strange thing happened that I was not aware of. They had a nice clock which only needed winding every thirty days and kept perfect time. Incredibly, the clock stopped at two minutes to four, the exact time that I was knocked down. Mum always thought that it was my destiny that these things would happen to me.

I used to dream that I was beautiful, completely whole and the life and soul of everywhere I went. I didn't realise that when you lose a limb it's like a bereavement and you go through similar things, depression, anger, grief. I just wanted to be like everyone else. Being twelve years old and with all the physical and emotional changes going on in my body, I just wanted to run and never stop, if only I had the energy. I could not concentrate at school, even though I wanted to do well. Looking back now, if I had just a smidgeon of confidence my life might have been different. At school I would say to myself, "Concentrate, concentrate", and I was so busy telling myself to do it that I couldn't hear what the teachers were saying and so I failed miserably in many subjects, except English.

I was taken to a psychiatrist but told no one about it: what a stigma! He wore a white coat, but I cannot remember him saying anything constructive to me. He seemed to speak more to Mum and I never really understood what he was trying to do for me. I wish I could have explained just how I felt, how odd, different and inferior. Nothing could change how I felt and I thought that this would be how my life would be forever. The days were very long and dark and I didn't know if I would ever feel any different. People were so kind but nothing they could say would help me. How pathetic this all sounds now, but I know anyone who has suffered from depression will understand how I felt.

I had a friend who lived across the road, whose dog just had some pups. I was asked if I would like one but living on the third floor of a tenement was not the ideal situation. Mum and Dad knew that it would be too much for me to look after, so I got a budgie instead. He was called Billy, he was beautiful and I loved him. He was hardly ever in his cage and he was a great diversion for me. We had him for many years and naturally I was distraught when he died.

Now my only solace was in music. My mum and dad bought me little record player, which looked like a small suitcase, and it was my saving grace. I saved up and started a record collection and stayed in my bedroom playing the same songs over and over again. My first record was by Elvis Presley singing 'His Latest Flame' and it was nearly worn through to the other side by the time I bought my next one. My favourite is Folk music, which came into my life many years later and it played a major part in my 'healing'.

My mum and dad were suffering too, but Mum was especially bad, as I suspect she was also suffering a nervous breakdown. She was advised by the doctor to take a job and so, much to our pleasure, she got a job at McDonalds biscuit factory. Every Thursday night she would bring back a bag of Penguins, Yo-Yo's and chocolate teacakes. At the same time Jenny was working as a comptometer operator in a biscuit factory and once a week she would bring home caramel wafers and other delights. At first we thought we were in chocolate heaven, but eventually we got slightly sick of them and longed for a plain tea biscuit.

My family bought me many toys and things to help me adapt to my new way of life, and one Christmas I was given something called 'Build It'. It was a fantastic thing, a forerunner of Lego, I think. There were sticks and cogs that allowed you to make wonderful things. My favourite was a Ferris Wheel that would stay erected for days until I tired of it and decided to build something else. My other favourite was a carousel which, when spun, would turn for a long time before slowing down. I don't know what happened to this toy but I'm sure my children would have loved it. I think my family were silently pleased that I was showing signs of being quite dexterous with my one hand, especially when it was quite fiddly and required lots of little sticks being inserted into cog-like rings.

I was going through what is now called 'a steep learning curve'. I learned to put rollers in my hair and did the same for my mum. I even succeeded in back-combing my hair. The other thing I loved was knitting. When I was in hospital, a lady tried to show me how to hold the knitting needles between my knees but I ended up with a great dent in my knee and an aching back! After I was fitted with my prosthesis, I knitted constantly as I could hold the needle under my arm – with no dents anywhere. The thing that really flummoxed me was putting on stockings and suspenders and until I could do this I had very colourful bruises on my thighs – thank goodness for tights.

Ellen was very good to me and would make me lovely clothes, knit beautiful cardigans and jumpers and I always loved everything she made for me. She also took me to the cinema many times and I remember how excited I was when she told me that she had tickets for the Glasgow premier of 'Ben Hur' and that one of the stars would be attending the performance. We hoped that it would be Charlton Heston but it turned out to be Stephen Boyd, who was a very good substitute as he made a very convincing 'baddie'.

I was always very self-conscious about my arm and so an incident that happened when I was in town with Ellen is etched on my mind. I was being taken to the cinema when my 'hand' fell off and rolled down the pavement. I was mortified and cried uncontrollably. Of course, my crying made everyone turn round to look. I made sure after that it was super-glued on.

There were more incidents like that many years later, but by then the sting had been taken out of it. One time I was at the butcher's counter in a large supermarket, busily talking to someone and when I left the queue a man chased after me saying, "Would this be yours?" He was holding my hand! At another time, I was standing at the back of the bus, waiting to get off, when, as I jumped, I heard a noise and looked down as my 'rogue appendage' fell off and rolled under the bus. It drove off and ran over my hand. In those days the artificial hands were made of a hard plastic and when I picked up my hand, which was gloved, I heard a jingling noise as all the fingers were broken into little pieces. I often wondered what the people in the Limb Fitting Centre thought of that.

I have only skirted around Mum and Dad's relationship as I feel that I would be betraying them to write much more. But the facts are true that every Friday night Dad would go out drinking and there would be an almighty row; then he would go out again on Saturday morning to his club and there would be another row on coming home at lunch time; and he would go out again on Saturday evening and would repeat the scenario. They would not speak to each other until Thursday, when the whole thing started again. Mum was obviously unhappy but could do nothing about the situation.

Dad always enjoyed going to the cinema, even by himself, and one evening was especially memorable. He went to see a John Wayne film at the local picture house and on arriving back home the doorbell rang and when the door was opened, an unopened packet of Spangles came flying through the air. When we asked if he enjoyed the film, his reply was that he would have enjoyed it more if he could have opened 'the bloomin' packet'. I know how disappointing it is to look forward to something, even as small as a sweet, and you're thwarted, you can't concentrate on anything else.

Apart from all the dramas, I still managed to have fun and a couple of incidents come to mind; I know Ellen will remember these with a smile. We were never very bothered about Guy Fawkes night, as it was a long walk to the back green from our flat and we could get a very good view of the firework displays from our flat. We were much more excited about some indoor fireworks that we bought in town. We waited until it was dark and set them up in the kitchen. We set the 'nose' of an elephant alight and waited until it suddenly took off. It must have been at least three feet long and we could hardly see in the kitchen for that smoke that was choking us. When Mum and Dad came back, we had to come up with an explanation fast!

The other little drama was when we bought a set of electric hair tongs. Ellen had long hair, so we tried them on her first. Unfortunately we left them in her hair too long and when we took them out she looked as if she was wearing a judge's wig. We howled with laughter until our stomachs hurt. It took three days for the single curl to straighten out.

Jenny and George were very also good to me and were

always taking me to the pictures. But George, being a joker would ask the conductor on the bus or tram for "Two tickets to town please". He would then look at me and say, "Where's your money?" knowing of course that I hadn't brought any. He would wink and say, "I'll pay for it this time, but the tickets are on you next time". I loved those visits to the cinema and I have grown up with such a knowledge of old movies that I'm not too bad at 'Trivial Pursuits', particularly on questions in the pink entertainment section.

I remember some good times involving Mum and Dad. She asked him to make her a new poker for the fire and as he worked with copper she knew he would make it well. We waited in anticipation for the new poker to arrive (how simple our lives were then – eager excitement at the prospect of a new poker!). It arrived and although it has grown by many inches during the years of telling, it took almost three if us to lift the blooming thing to poke the fire. He also made us a copper hot water bottle but it only cooled down around four o'clock in the morning, so it was almost time to get up before we could warm our toes.

We had a coal fire that was sometimes a devil to light. We would hold a piece of newspaper against it to draw the flames up, so Dad made us a copper sheet with a handle to use in place of newspaper. However, by the time the fire was glowing, so was the handle and we had to get a wet towel to pull it away.

With four women in the house, Dad didn't have to lift a finger, as we all had our allotted chores. Every Sunday, cakes would be baked while he watched the television and he would be given a bowl with butter and sugar in it and we had great delight in telling him to 'beat it'. It was just as well we were never in a hurry for the mixture because he would sit slowly stirring it. I was always sent in to have a peak to see how it was coming along.

I was very fortunate that to take my mind off things, my parents rented our first television. We would all gather round every Sunday evening trying to answer the questions on the quiz shows. I remember one that was called 'Dotto' in which famous faces were blanked out and as the dots were joined up, whoever could recognize a face the quickest, won. My Dad always shouted "President Eisenhower"; it never was, in all the years we watched. I can still recall a lot of the original adverts on the TV, for instance 'The Esso sign means happy motoring', 'Mazda Lamps stay brighter longer', the ice block in which a tube of SR toothpaste was frozen, and so on.

I have a mind that accumulates utter trivia but it also harbours things that I would like to erase; but if you have imagination, you don't get to choose what you retain or forget. I remember watching the TV and being horrified to see a documentary on the relief of Belsen Concentration Camp. I know that every person should be made to watch these things, but I have never managed to erase those pictures from my mind. I have seen many things over the years I would rather not have seen, but the mind does not discern the good memories from the bad.

A good imagination is both wonderful and awful. I remember my schoolteachers telling us of William Wallace and how he was hanged, drawn and quartered. Even at that young age I could sort of picture this in my mind, although fortunately it didn't conjure up the proper picture. When the film 'Braveheart' came out, I couldn't watch it because of the ending. I know film-goers just go and enjoy the movie, but I can only think of what the person actually went through and cannot erase the images from my mind.

Although school was a bit daunting for me, I enjoyed being with my friends and I could have fun. When I was about fifteen I remember two girls sitting behind me talking about the make-up they were going to buy and what colour lipstick would suit them. When they came into the classroom the following Monday, they each brought in a lipstick by Yardley, called 'Pink Magic' and it had the most wonderful perfume. I thought I'd save up my pocket money and buy the same lipstick. It was my favourite for many years.

During this time I was still feeling very down. Although, looking back, it was my spirit that was down and not my physical condition, Mum decided to try a tonic for me that she hoped would do me good. It was called 'Sanatogen' and it had the consistency and taste of wallpaper paste. I was forced to drink this every evening and even now I can feel my stomach heaving at the memory. Please, no more tonics!

When I was sixteen, the time came to go to work. I was dreading it, as I was comfortable in my own environment and was loathe to step out of it. I had been to night school to continue my shorthand, which I enjoyed. I managed to attain 140 words per minute, but who would employ me? At that time, you left school on Friday and started work on Monday. Just before I left school on the Friday afternoon, my music teacher, Mrs Kidd, asked me if I would like to have a career in music, as she thought I had a good voice. How could I? I would surely have to hide behind everyone in a concert!

In any event, it was too late, because the school had arranged a job interview for me on the last day of term and

I got an immediate place as an office junior in a large paint works. With great trepidation I travelled on my own on the bus and entered the huge company office. When I saw all the glamorous secretaries, wearing their beautiful clothes with such self-assurance and confidently chatting to each other, I felt even more insecure. However, I was very fortunate in that I was operating the telephone in a booth that was hidden away from everyone, so nobody could see me. When I think back, I must have looked such a fright wearing a pair of oversized earphones and a sort of trumpet-shaped device on my chest. I loved operating the telephone exchange with its little numbers on flaps that dropped down when you connected the callers. It was great fun. After a few weeks I found that I could chat to the customers who called, knowing they could not see how I looked. I thoroughly enjoyed my time in that little telephone booth. I began to have the confidence even to start some repartee with them because, of course, they could not see me. I was there for six months.

By this time Jenny and her husband, George, had moved to Irvine in Ayrshire, and Ellen and I went to visit them most weekends. George was still a bit of a joker and we all got on so well. We had great fun and I felt 'normal' with no pressure to be anything but myself. I even managed to go to some dances with them, organised through Jenny's work. I was very anxious and couldn't believe it when someone asked me to dance. It was one of the chaps who worked in the Limb Fitting Centre that I attended, so he made me feel that I could relax. Those happy days are forever etched in my mind and I shall never forget them. We all still get on so well to this day.

My brother George had married. His wife Rena

worked in an office in the centre of Glasgow, and they were looking for an office junior who could type. I enjoyed typing and applied and got the job. I felt so much better working with my sister-in-law, because we were always laughing and she was wonderful at telling me of the films she had seen; I knew the entire script of 'West Side Story' before I saw the film. We worked together for many happy years. I made very good friends in that office, most of whom I still contact to this day.

I had a very good friend called Ann, who I met at school. She was from the Isle of Skye. Her father had died and her mother and brothers and sisters had to move from their home to find work. I always wondered how they could settle in a huge city like Glasgow after living on a quiet island like Skye, but the brothers all got jobs quickly and they appeared to cope. We seemed to gel very quickly and would walk to school together, share our dreams and silly girly thoughts and I felt very comfortable with her family. She had three sisters and three brothers and at last I felt I could chat to people and not feel different.

We went to the cinema twice a week and I loved every minute of the films we saw. We went to the same films over and over again, especially 'GI Blues', starring Elvis Presley. Both of us were terrible gigglers and many a time the usherette would shine her torch on us, saying "Keep quiet you two or out you go!" Why did that make us giggle even more? We went shopping in town, where I could be hidden in the crowds and feel that no one could see my artificial arm. I had no idea that I was not at fault for what had happened to me, but I felt that I should cover up. Looking back, I would have given anything to have been brave enough to go out without wearing long sleeves in summer.

When I was sixteen, I suddenly developed hay fever. What a glamorous condition! As if I didn't look odd enough – all I needed were red eyes and nose. A few months later I sneezed so much that I burst a blood vessel in my throat while at work and blood was shooting all over my typewriter and desk. It was quite spectacular. My boss drove me to the A&E and I was X-rayed. It was a bit scary but eventually it stopped. Three weeks later the hospital wrote to say that there was something odd about the X-ray and could I possibly go back for them to check?

They told me I had tuberculosis. More visits to the NHS. For the next two years, four times a day, I had to swallow a packet of what looked like the little cake decorations, 'hundreds and thousands', although they were not quite as sweet. I could hardly get them down as they got stuck between my teeth and when you accidentally crunched them, they tasted awful. I tried water, milk, lemonade, Lucozade, but nothing made them any easier to swallow. I often asked at the hospital why couldn't they be put in tablet form, but I don't remember being given a satisfactory answer. To this day there are certain drinks that bring back memories of that 'budgie seed', as my nephew called it.

I was having very strange pains in my leg which I couldn't quite explain and was sent again to hospital. They found a huge piece of glass that was embedded in my leg and had started to move. It was removed and so I had another scar. I find it hard to believe but, unknown to me, Mum kept this bit of glass in a jar in the cupboard for years.

Another trip to hospital was quite an ordeal. After work one Friday night I told my Mum that I had had a pain in my stomach all day. After a sandwich, I went to the doctor's and sat in the queue for a long time, as you used to do. When I saw him, he immediately phoned the hospital and I said I had to have my appendix out. I wasn't too worried because by now the NHS and I were well acquainted. I turned up at the hospital and was asked if I had anything to eat in the last hour, so, of course I had to say "Yes". I was whisked off to a bed with the curtains drawn round and a trolley on which was an implement that looked like a medieval instrument of torture. It was. I had to have my stomach pumped in a procedure that was so unpleasant I'll never forget it.

I have never thought to ask, 'Why does all this happen to me?' I think, deep down, that I have been fortunate to be able accept the things that I could not change, which is a blessing, since you really can't do anything but accept. When I was going back to the hospital for a checkup I was in a lift with a few other people when I heard a man complaining bitterly that when he lost one of his fingers in an accident at work, and his whole life was in decline because he couldn't catch a ball with one hand. I thought, I could teach you a few tricks. The only thing I wanted to do, but cannot, is to play the guitar. But I always have the cheek to say that had I been able to do so, I would have been outstandingly good at it.

After the appendix operation I was off work for about six weeks and was terrified that my boss would find someone else to take my place. When I went back to work there was some else in MY office, but she was actually a very nice girl of about my age, but very much more outgoing. She didn't stay long as she soon found a better job. I couldn't understand it; there wasn't a better job than this one!

Chapter 3

My sister Ellen had not been well for quite a while after my accident, also suffering from post-traumatic stress. It seemed to last so long for both of us that the family decided that she and I would go on holiday. We were going to be terribly adventurous and go to Italy. My friend Ann was asked and my cousin Margaret, with whom I got on famously.

Of course I was terrified of flying and as soon as the door was closed with a bang, I wanted to get off. Ellen had to keep me pinned down in the seat. I think that the air hostesses could sense my fear and before I knew what was happening, I was invited to join the captain in the cockpit. It was wonderful and I was quite overwhelmed with what I saw, being level with the big fluffy clouds. We were flying into the dark and when we looked out of the window, which I had to work up the nerve to do, I saw cities lit up, looking like fairyland. I settled down in my seat after that exciting experience.

We had a wonderful time in Italy. Way back in the Sixties it was still quite unusual to go abroad, so we felt very special. However, I had not really thought about sunbathing on the beach. I hadn't worn a swimming costume since I was taught to swim when I was about ten, so I took to wearing a blouse over my swimsuit until I could lie down and look like everybody else on the beach.

The holiday was filled with new experiences. I had never before eaten pizza at two o'clock in the morning, nor had I eaten spaghetti. That was another steep learning curve – do not eat pasta when you are wearing a white blouse. We also went to an outdoor cinema to see 'From Russia with Love'; fortunately we had seen it back home, or we would never have known what it was about. Sean Connery's voice had been dubbed in an extremely high-pitched voice which was quite disconcerting and it somehow took the romance out of it. But it was a wonderful experience, a whole new world. Shops were open at all hours of the night. The most beautiful clothes shops beckoned us in, which we did, and we had a wonderful time. Apart from the pasta, we also enjoyed a banana split at two o'clock in the morning. I'd like to try that now – I think. It was the first time I had tasted wine. It was alright, but orange juice was more in my line.

On coming back from holiday, I found that some of my friends had boyfriends. I thought that I would feel slightly envious or jealous, but I did not. I knew that for certain I would never have a boyfriend and that I did not want one, as I would certainly get hurt. I had gone through enough emotional stress and I definitely did not want any more, thank you very much.

I thoroughly enjoyed my job and felt that I was good at what I was doing. The company made a lubrication system that was used in the QE2 and so the business was doing well, so well in fact that an American company was showing interest. A huge Texan came over to visit my boss. He arrived at lunch time when I was knitting an Aran sweater. He just stood and looked at me for a minute or two and said in a lovely drawl, "Well I'll be damned!" This gentleman came over many times and we got on very well.

We were all devastated when we heard that he, his wife and the captain had disappeared completely in their boat; lost, would you believe it, in the Bermuda Triangle.

I am very fortunate in that I can accept every situation I find myself in, so by this time I was quite happy with my life. I was eighteen, I had a good job, I played all the music I loved, so what else did I need? One day I was walking through the stores department at work and did not notice a handsome young man standing there. He had come for a job interview, which he got. His name was Gilbert and we always seemed to be yelling at each other, in a fun sort of way. After some months working together, I found myself being drawn to him but there was no way I was going to fall for anyone, as I thought they would only feel sorry for me. He asked me out twice and I refused. He asked once more and then I gave in, although he later told me that he was so sure I was going to refuse again, that when he said "Are you doing anything tonight?" and I said "No", he said immediately, "Well, can I take you out tomorrow?"

I was still very self-conscious about my arm, even though he saw me every day for months. We went to the cinema and I hardly said a word, thinking to myself, 'Do not get hurt'. He drove me home and didn't ask me out again and I thought, I was right, he did feel sorry for me. But at the weekend he turned up at my door and took me to the seaside. I now felt much more comfortable with him and I could relax and enjoy myself; and so began the next part of my life.

At that time, no one in our family had a car, so that was another thing Mum could worry about. Gilbert and I did not seem to set up dates, he usually just turned up for me. It was a bit disconcerting, as he called once when we were all decorating and I looked 'delightful' in my working clothes. We used to go to Loch Lomond and around the Trossachs and I saw many wonderful places that were new to me. I was having a whale of a time. His grandmother on his father's side lived in Gretna and we occasionally went down to see her. She look like a Dowager Duchess and, guess what, I was terrified of her. I later learned that she had gone a bit 'funny' and was lighting the fire with five pound notes from her handbag. I think there was a great rush by her family down to Gretna to stop this from happening again. Gilbert had lots of friends and I felt very comfortable with all of them. His family welcomed me and his sister and brother and I got on really well.

When Gilbert told me he loved me, I couldn't believe it. He told me that on the day he came for the interview, he didn't notice my arm, just me. We got engaged after a year and I was so happy. How could this happen to me? He bought me a beautiful engagement ring and I couldn't wait to show it off. We planned our wedding for the next year and started to save as much as possible. I didn't know how Mum and Dad really felt about my engagement. They didn't jump up and down with excitement, but then they never did, so I hoped they were happy for us. I think they still looked on me as their 'little girl'.

Gilbert's mum's name was Christina but she was called Bunty – I still don't know why. She was a real sweetie. We got on extremely well as she and I both lived in a sort of fantasy world. As soon as any problems cropped up we would drift into the world of movies and favourite books. Gilbert's dad was a very clever chap but I always felt intimidated by him; I don't know why, because he was always very nice to me, but I felt that he and I never got to know each other as well as we could have done.

Gilbert's brother Keith and his sister Marilyn became very good friends with me and we got on famously. We often went out in a crowd and had such a laugh. But I was still feeling very vulnerable, so imagine my horror when in a café one night, I was standing looking round for a table, when this 'poser' of a young man came up to me and said, right in my face, "You need hands", which was the title of a song by Max Bygraves. I was stunned and totally distraught. Some of the lads in our crowd had heard him and it took all our strength to hold them back from chasing him out of the café.

Sadly, incidents like that can set you back so much and I felt totally deflated and cried for a few nights afterwards. How could anyone be so cruel? Unfortunately I have come across many people like that man, who think that they're extremely smart in putting you down. One woman I recall called me a one-armed bandit on our first meeting, which took my breath away. Incredibly, I met her about twenty years later and she said exactly the same thing! Fortunately my skin had got very much thicker since the first occasion and I could let it go.

We set the date for our wedding, 5th October 1968, almost ten years after my accident. It was difficult to find a wedding dress that would cover up the harness of my arm, since all the styles showed above the neckline. I asked the limb fitting department many times if they could fix the harness so that it would be covered up, but to no avail. My sister Ellen, who then lived in Sheffield, was very gifted in everything creative and she offered to make my wedding dress. So, off I went to Sheffield and we had great fun choosing a pattern and material. It was a coat dress with buttons down the front and a high neck, just what I wanted; it was beautiful.

On the morning of the wedding I went into town to have my hair done, leaving at around nine o'clock and hoping to be back by around noon. But of course, 'the best laid plans ... gang aft agley'. I had very long hair at the time and had decided to have it put up, which took more time than usual. Then the bus broke down on the way back home and I had to wait for over an hour for another one. So I returned home at about two o'clock to find my mum hanging out of the window looking for me, absolutely frantic and thinking that something had gone wrong or that I decided to run off. Fortunately the wedding ceremony was scheduled for 5.30 p.m., late in the afternoon because Rangers and Celtic were playing at Ibrox Park, just along the road from the church and transport would be at a standstill around five o'clock.

Jenny and George's daughter, Ailson, and Gilbert's sister, Marilyn, were my bridesmaids and they both looked beautiful in their lovely blue dresses. We had a wonderful wedding reception with lots of fun and laughter, although my dear mum cried from the time I got up in the morning until I waved goodbye in the evening. Many years later I found the receipt for our wedding reception and was amazed to see that the whole event for about sixty people, including drinks, food and all the trappings for a lovely day, cost £169.00.

I had never been to London, so we decided to go and do all the 'touristy things'. Gilbert's aunt and uncle, George and Jean, lived in Haywards Heath and we went to visit them. We arrived at their beautiful big house, which made me feel so intimidated again. I heard a strange noise when we entered, which Gilbert explained was their pet African Grey parrot. His Uncle George worked as an insurance broker for Lloyds of London and Jean and he had worked all over the world. When they lived in Nigeria, they mentioned to their houseboy that they would love a bird as a companion, and the next thing they knew they were presented with a baby bird (something that is not allowed today). They named the parrot 'Tweetie Pie'. He had his own certificates to travel by plane. I soon discovered that he loved to chew laces straight from your shoes, or your toes if shoes were not available. I noticed that the wonderful oak doors throughout the house had a sort of scalloped edging on the top. They explained that the parrot liked to sit on top of the doors whistling and biting chunks out of the woodworks. What could he do with fingers?

We were supposed to stay in London for two weeks, but since Gilbert's work was piling up we felt that we had to cut our honeymoon short, although we had a fantastic time. On returning to Glasgow, we were told by the wedding photographer that something had happened to his camera and all we could have were the black and white 'proofs'. These were the photos that you wouldn't choose for your album, so they are not on show very often.

We had put a deposit on a new house which was still being built, and so we lived for six months in a flat not far from my office. The flat was really just a huge room in one of the many substantial red sandstone buildings that Glasgow is famous for. We had to use a communal kitchen, in which we were allocated a cooker and a sink … and heaven help us if we used the wrong one!

The last few years had been the happiest of my life. Gilbert's business was doing very well and I loved my job, what more could I ask for? When I first met Gilbert he was a bit of a daredevil at driving, so it was no surprise to learn that he was going to go in for something called Autocross. I was happy to go along with this but didn't realise just how financially and emotionally costly it would become. We travelled all over Scotland and I thoroughly enjoyed going to all the race meetings, making many new friends. Not surprisingly, Gilbert was fantastic, winning practically every race he entered (we still have the silver cups to prove it. I have to polish them – Silvo is just as bad as Brasso!).

We were invited to stay with Ellen and Graham for a short break. When we arrived, we discovered that George and Rena, and Jenny and George were staying near Blackpool for a holiday, so the four of us went to meet them at the seaside. We had a whale of a time going on all the rides and doing fun fair things. We went into the 'House of Fun', which consisted of lots of obstacles you had to clamber over and moving planks that you had to walk on, whilst trying to keep your dignity; I think we all left ours at the door. When we got to the last obstacle there was a huge slide – you had to sit on a mat and come zipping down. Well Jenny, Ellen, Rena and I decided we'd rather not, thank you very much, but my brother-in-law George was going to show these lily-livered ladies how it was done.

We walked down the stairs and waited for him at the bottom, waving to him as he set off on his mat. At the centre of the slide there was a slight bump, which the children enjoyed because they flew in the air and came down with a bump, but when we saw George's face, which had turned a strange colour, we knew the children were having a better time than he was. That was not the end of our giggling, because poor George was trying to slow himself down on his 'flight' down, using his heels as brakes, but as he was wearing sandals the slide burned two holes in his socks. It might be a small exaggeration but we were sure that he walked round Blackpool with wisps of smoke coming from his feet. I also think that his back has never been the same since.

After three years of Gilbert working all hours of the day and night, the area in which his garage was located was bulldozed to make way for new housing. This affected his business, as most of his customers were from around the area. Things became slightly more difficult financially. Then I found that I was pregnant and amongst my feelings of joy was the thought, 'How can we afford this?'. I knew that I could learn to do everything that a baby needed, but finances were a real worry. I did not tell anyone at work that I was expecting a baby, so it was a shock to them when I was rushed into hospital with a threatened miscarriage. My situation was revealed on the sick note that I had to send into work. On top of all this we were devastated when my boss died suddenly; he was only in his late forties. Things were never really the same when he died but I still felt a great pang of sorrow when I had to leave.

One Saturday a few weeks after I left work, Gilbert was working late as usual. He came home around ten-thirty in the evening and said that when he had been grinding a piece of metal a small fragment had got stuck in his eye. I dashed upstairs, put my coat on and rushed Gilbert down to the Western Infirmary. As we were driving there I suddenly noticed that I had not put on my 'hand', but on this occasion I wasn't bothered. The hospital on a Saturday night was always full of merry party-goers. There was a very large queue in the A&E department and I was standing there saying, 'Another encounter with the good old NHS', when the young man in front of me, who had a dirty tea towel wrapped round his badly bleeding hand, looked at his hand, looked at my empty sleeve, looked at me and said "You're in worse shape than I am hen, so you can go first". True!

At this time we bought a dog, a white English Bull Terrier that we called 'Mac'. Gilbert had one when he was a boy and had fond memories of it. Mac was a very sturdy, strong dog, and Gilbert took him to work for security. I found him quite difficult to handle. I looked after him well, but he took me for a walk rather than the other way around. He was a bit of a devil, learning how to get into the fridge and eating the sausages that were meant for our dinner that night. Since cash was in very short supply, I remember chasing him around the lounge with a pair of scissors trying to cut off the last two before he swallowed them. When he had his 'mad half hour' of an evening, he would gallop round the room, his feet getting further and further off the floor, so before I redecorated, there were dog paw prints just about a foot down from the ceiling that had to be washed off.

Money was terribly short and of course this caused many problems. As the old saying goes, 'Love goes out the window, when poverty marches through the door', and that's exactly what happened. Gilbert was still racing and I think that it took his mind off the situation we were in. This went on for two years until one day Gilbert was offered a job in a big established motor company. I thought this would be the answer to our problems, but unfortunately it had quite the opposite effect on the situation. It was my problem, and only mine, but his new job meant that he was at home much more and I felt that he was encroaching on my territory. I knew it was unfair, but I was convinced that our problems were all my fault and I could feel the old feelings of inferiority creeping back.

I was really disappointed that during my pregnancy I didn't have the cravings I had heard about. I'm sure I would have liked to gnaw on a piece of coal but I was very lucky to sail through the rest of my pregnancy without much bother. Unfortunately I had a very long labour and I remember the staff nurse and the doctor quarrelling as they stood over me. I heard the nurse say, "She has too much acetone in her", and I thought, I use acetone to take off my nail polish. Then the doctor said something like, "We'll give her a buckle". Good grief! I was to be tortured! But thirty-six hours later my daughter was born.

When I saw Adele, it was love at first sight. I used to lie in the hospital bed and stare at her. I coped very well, much better than I thought and I always prided myself on the fact that I never stabbed her once with a nappy pin – in those days we used Terry nappies and gauze squares. She was a tiny little thing, weighing only five and a half pounds when born and she looked like a little doll. There's always a way of doing things and although I had one arm I found looking after her quite easy. The difficult thing was putting her socks on, for every time I tried she would spread her little toes out.

For the next two years Gilbert and I struggled on, growing apart, but I did not contemplate separation or anything – where on earth would I go? Also, I didn't want to admit to the family that I was a failure because, after all, I believed it was my fault. I think my problem was, and probably always has been, that I had lived a sort of fantasy world where Prince Charming would come along and make me feel the way I wanted to feel. Poor Gilbert had no chance.

Gilbert's sister told me that she knew of a job for a clerk-typist in Gartnavel Hospital, a hospital for the mentally ill. There was also a crèche for the staff's children. I applied, thinking that this would surely help the situation. When I went for the interview, I was rather confused as there were two hospitals in the same grounds. One was a beautiful new building, all light and airy, and the other was a dark red brick building that looked similar to the house in the 'Amityville Horror' story. Guess which one the job was in – yes, the latter.

I was greeted by the head of the department, who asked if liked Country and Western music. I said "Yes, I like most kinds of music". I didn't know too many Country and Western artists, but she said "If you can type, the job is yours". I was taken on and I loved it. I met the most fabulous people, so outgoing and funny. There were always concerts they went to, inviting me along. Sometimes I could arrange for a baby-sitter and I joined in the fun. We went to a concert to see Johnny Cash and although I didn't know much about Country and Western music before I went in, I did when I came out. Hearing that music today brings back wonderful memories. On Fridays we would all go to the local pub for lunch and one day we sat down beside a scruffy looking chap with a beard, who turned out to be Billy Connolly, although he wasn't as famous then as he is now. We had heard him singing in a folk club with his friend Gerry Rafferty and we all decided that he was no singer, but he was extremely funny – before all the swearing crept into his act.

Adele was only two but she loved the crèche and she was quite a hit with the staff. It was the most wonderful job

I ever had. It was a full-time job, working in the printing department in the morning and the engineering department in the afternoon. In the engineering department I worked with thirty men, all of whom had a wonderful sense of humour. I knew they were very protective of me and I felt that I was looked after by my friends.

On the first day that I started the job, I was walking back from the crèche to the office when I met a chap doing some gardening. I wasn't aware that the patients would be working in the hospital grounds and when he said to me, "Do you know I was murdered three years ago?", I had no idea what to say to him. So I asked him, "How are you now?" and walked away very quickly.

When I arrived at the printing department I was shown into a tiny office with three chairs, one desk and a window, through which you could see the patients working. I thought it was wonderful that the day patients could go home every evening and then come to work every day. What a shame this does not happen anymore. Some of the patients were very lucid and we had many conversations, sharing jokes with them.

On the other hand, there were some that I was very wary of. For a 'treat' I was taken up to the very oldest part of the hospital and was taken into a padded cell. My goodness! If you weren't demented before, you certainly would be after being in there for a while. It was horrendous. When you spoke, there was no reverberation in your ears, no echo, nothing – I never went back.

There were some very sad cases amongst the patients I met in the printing department. I was told that one of the ladies who worked with us every day had been raped when she was fifteen by the master of the house where she worked as a laundry maid. When she fell pregnant, she was put into the 'hospital', the baby was taken away from her and she had been there ever since. It was heartbreaking.

The engineering department where I worked in the afternoons was completely different. The chief engineer was a man with a wandering eye but fortunately it did not wander to me. The storeman, Alex, was fantastic. He had a quick wit like my brother George and I'm sure if you are in the company of someone witty like that, your own wit seems to be honed somewhat. We had a wonderful time. I even enjoyed the work I had to do, although the typing often interfered with the fun I was having.

I felt happy when I left for work every morning because I could leave all the money troubles behind me. My salary made things easier, but we were in debt and it would take something very special to happen to sort things out. I loved my job so much because I could leave my house in the morning and step into a world where I was accepted, enjoy wonderful company and feel that I was loved. It was just what I wanted but unfortunately it made me feel even more resentful when going home. I know it seems selfish, but all I wanted was something that Gilbert seemed to be unable to give me – affection. Yet, knowing his background, I should have understood that it's impossible to teach someone to demonstrate a feeling that they have never experienced themselves.

We didn't have much time or money for holidays but when Adele was about five years old, we managed two weeks' holiday in Cornwall. We went with George and Rena and their two daughters, Lesley and Kathryn, and we had a wonderful time playing badminton on the beach and exploring the beautiful county.

We didn't have another holiday for many years and when we did we always went with Gilbert's mum. Her sister Jean had a huge holiday caravan at a place called Maidens near Girvan in Ayrshire. We went with Bunty for many years and she was very good company and a wonderful cook, so I didn't mind being the chief bottle washer. The caravan was near Culzean (pronounced 'Culane') Castle and there were many beautiful grounds to walk in. It was also right on the beach, which was wonderful for Adele.

Some months after starting work in the hospital, Gilbert picked Adele and me up from work in his van. He had the dog in the back. When we got into the house the dog attacked Adele without warning. Fortunately, Gilbert managed to pull him off but we knew she had been hurt. It all happened so quickly that we did not immediately see that a part of her ear was lying on the carpet. We rushed her to hospital with the bit of ear in a bag full of ice. We then had to take her to Canniesburn Hospital, which deals with plastic surgery and burns. We watched as she was taken on a trolley into the theatre, looking so terribly tiny. Later we were told that the ear could not be repaired but we were so thankful that she had not been hurt more badly. My heart was breaking. We had the dog put down before visiting her the next day.

One incident I shall never forget was when we went to visit her and she was sitting on a bed playing cars with a young boy. She was facing us so we could only see his back, and when he turned round, he had no face, just the most beautiful brown eyes I've seen. We found out that he had been playing in an old scrap car and had put a match into the petrol tank He was horribly burned. Adele was playing and talking to him as best she could at the age of two, without even noticing what we had been shocked by. Very young children have that wonderful capacity to look beyond disfigurement.

The final chapter of this incident was when I took Adele to hospital for a last checkup. She was sitting on my knee as the consultant was talking to me and he kept looking at me in an inquisitive way. He then said, 'What is that on your face?'. I told him that it was a chickenpox scar from many years back, but that it was tingling and was slightly bigger than before. He took an enormous magnifying glass, held it up to my face and said, "You have a rodent ulcer, would you like me to remove it for you?". I said "Do you think I should?", to which he answered, "Come tomorrow at 8.30 a.m.". I did and he removed it. I thought, Oh no! Something else to make me feel different. I had eight tiny stitches right in the middle of my cheek, but he must have been a very good embroiderer, because they are barely discernible.

My sister had married a very nice chap from Sheffield, called Graham, the year before we were married. He was a manager of a large motor dealership. He contacted Gilbert to tell him that there was a job in the Rally Sport department and would he be interested in it? We had been down to stay with them many times and I thought it was really lovely where they lived. So Gilbert said "Yes" and went down for an interview. My other sister Jenny and her husband had been made redundant in Scotland and were staying with Ellen and Graham for a short break. Luckily there was a job vacancy in British Steel that Jenny's husband applied for and he got the job.

So my older sister was moving to Sheffield. Did I want to do the same? Naturally, I did not want to leave my wonderful job at the hospital and all my friends. By this time Adele was at school and was quite settled and I didn't want to disrupt her. But something at the back of my mind told me that we would go. I was really resentful of Gilbert because he was making me leave a job I loved.

Gilbert went down to Sheffield, living with Ellen and Graham for a few months, travelling back to Glasgow at the weekends. I was left to try to sell the house. Tricky, but I did it. I think Mum and Dad were a bit sad to see all their girls moving away, but a least we would be together. A few weeks later, Gilbert's father was taken ill and was in hospital. Bunty did not actually say, but she implied that he had cancer. He died suddenly, just six short weeks after the cancer was discovered.

Gilbert and his father had a very volatile relationship when he was a boy, but I think that because his dad had been a powerful influence in his life, Gilbert was devastated when he died. When we are young, we think our parents are immortal. Gilbert's dad was also called Gilbert. He had lived in Gretna for many years, as did the whole family before moving to Glasgow. So when his father passed away the family decided to have him buried in Gretna, near his own parents. I felt sad that we hadn't got to know each other better.

Gilbert's father was a refrigeration engineer and Gilbert once told me of a time when they both went to a hospital in Newcastle to help install a refrigeration unit in a new mortuary. I've been told many times how creepy it was to be there after everyone had gone home. His dad also was involved in the engineering side of an aerodrome during the war. We never found out exactly what he did.

I think I might have blotted my copybook at the

funeral, as I was sitting next to a friend of Gilbert's at the lunch after the service. He had the most fantastic sense of humour, but after the pudding had been served, he stated in a loud voice that the plum crumble would 'draw the cheeks of your a… together'. I had to pretend to pick up my napkin from the floor, but unfortunately I was down there for more time than it would normally take, trying to collect myself; so I very sheepishly looked round, only to find Keith standing over me asking if he could come and sit at our table.

Our move to Sheffield was not without its traumas. The three of us travelled behind the furniture van in a little Mini estate car that was packed to the roof with all the last-minute things to be taken. We were just out of Glasgow when Adele started to cry. I asked her what was wrong and she said that she had left her hula hoop behind; could we go back? I promised to buy her a new one but unfortunately I did not get around to it for some time, and even to this day she will remind me how 'cruel' I was to her.

It was winter and as we were nearing Carlisle, snow started to fall thick and fast and we suddenly realised that we were the only car on the road. We were supposed to arrive in Sheffield at nine o'clock, but at ten o'clock we were stuck on the A66 just before Scotch Corner in a car with a very sick engine. Gilbert and I tried pushing it up to the top of the hill just to see if it would start up again, but it was no good. He knew exactly what was wrong – a cracked distributor cap – but it wasn't something he could fix as we had no spare. The snow was so heavy and deep by this time that our trousers were soaked. The only thing we could do was wrap up in plastic bin bags and wait.

About an hour later a Land Rover passed by and we called out to the driver to ask if he could call the police to see if we could get a tow off the road. He said he would and we waited and waited. As he drove past us, he told us that the A66 had been closed from Carlisle and that was why there was no other traffic on the road. Eventually the police arrived and telephoned a nearby bed and breakfast and booked us in. By this time it was three o'clock in the morning.

They drove us to the guesthouse and knocked on the door – no answer. They knocked harder and a lady in her dressing gown and with curlers in her hair opened the door, only to say that no one had called her. Now that she had been woken up, what was the problem? Apparently it was another guesthouse further along the road! Feeling rather guilty, the three of us went up to a freezing cold bedroom, searching our pockets for coins for the gas heater. The only person able to sleep that night was Adele. Very fortunately the place we were staying at had a garage next to it and our car was soon fixed. We hadn't been able to contact Ellen and Graham in Sheffield, so they were rather frantic until we managed to call them the next morning. No mobile phones in those days.

We stayed with Ellen and Graham for three months before finding a house of our own at Dronfield, a lovely part of the country just on the edge of the Peak District. We loved our new, big, bright house and, best of all, the huge garage that was big enough for Gilbert to work in at the weekend. But things did not improve in our relationship. I had convinced myself that everything was my fault and my old inferiority complex crept up on me again. I am convinced that when you have been deep in a dark place, even although it was many years before, the same inadequacy creeps over you and then, all at once, inferiority jumps up and bites you.

However, something really good happened in December 1979, when I took driving lessons and passed first time, although when I phoned Gilbert to tell him, he said he would only believe it when he saw the piece of paper. My test had not been easy because in the week before the test, my driving instructor was being tested and during my lessons I had his examining officer sitting behind me, testing my instructor. My instructor asked the examiner if he had any tips for my test. Looking at the steering knob I had to use, he said "You must have both hands on the wheel". I thought, that'll be clever! So Gilbert and I went to the limb fitting hospital to ask for another steering wheel knob. They fitted it and I went for my driving test. I was following the examiner's directions when he said "Please turn left" and my coat sleeve caught on the other steering knob. I couldn't turn the wheel and we came face to face with a bus. I had to say, "Your Mr So-and-so told me I had to have both hands on the steering wheel, so it's all his fault." Happily the examiner said "Let's start again", which we did, and I passed.

I was now able to visit Ellen, who didn't work, and we had a fantastic time every time we met. We have the same sense of humour and have been known to have to stop the car at the side of the road to wipe away the tears of laughter. I don't know what my life would have been like if she and I hadn't got together once or twice a week. I can guarantee that Ellen was not aware of how I was really feeling.

I suppose that when you feel that everything is possibly your own fault, you don't really want to admit there is anything wrong. I have always thought that I have quite a sunny disposition and have been told so a few times, but I never thought that I could feel such a strong resentment, bordering on what I thought could be hatred, for Gilbert. All I wanted from him was a hug now and again, but he just didn't know how. It would have made my life much more bearable if we could have shared our feelings and talked about the problems we had, but as soon as a topic was broached that touched a nerve, the shutters would come down and that was the end of the discussion. I felt I was trying to break down a brick wall.

Although I was so unhappy, Gilbert was not aware of how I felt as he was trying to keep food on the table. Before I got married I had been given some compensation for my accident. It seemed like a fortune back then, but now it seems a paltry sum. But I always had beautiful clothes and tried to be as fashionable as I could; now I couldn't afford a T-shirt from the market. I blame myself for some of the resentment that was hanging over us. We couldn't tell the family that we were struggling financially, although I'm sure they would have helped if they had known. It was the time when bank interest rates were around fifteen percent and life was really a struggle.

I decided that I had had enough. I packed a bag, not knowing where Adele and I were going. I went up to the bedroom and with a heavy heart, I prayed for the first time in many years. I said "God, if you are really there, please help me". In the quiet of my room, I felt I heard a voice saying "Yes". I was afraid, so much so that I didn't want to look round because I knew He was standing beside me. I felt the concrete slab that had been sitting on my chest for years, disappear immediately. I KNEW everything would be alright. I was so sure that anyone who looked at me would notice immediately. I don't know how long I stayed there, it could have been two weeks for all I knew, but I didn't want to stop this most amazing experience. I knew instantly that I was in the company of God. Who else could have taken this burden from me at a single asking?

For the first time in many years I looked forward to Gilbert coming home. We did not run into each other's arms like Heathcliffe and Cathy, but I felt so elated that this was the way it should have been for all the previous years. Gilbert could see that there was a change in our relationship but I knew he would never say anything. I woke up the next morning with such a light heart. I hadn't felt that way for so many years and I looked forward to starting another chapter in my life with the man I fell in love with.

I had been suffering very bad muscle pains in my stump and was sent to many different departments in different hospitals without finding the cause. I contacted the surgeon who had operated on me in Glasgow. He remembered me and arranged for me to go up to Scotland as soon as possible.

I did and was operated on again. The next day, in a very sad state, I went home to Dronfield by train. The surgery seemed to have worked but after a few months it was back to the way it had been. After about a year I couldn't stand it anymore, so back I went to my own doctor and started the process all over again. I was sent to one consultant who didn't quite understand how painful it really was. He grabbed hold of my stump and kneaded it to check where the pain was. When I climbed down from the ceiling, I said, "Yes, that's where the pain is!", but he could not do anything for me and I was sent to a neurosurgeon, whose manner was quite different. He took a piece of cotton wool, ran it down my stump and told me to tell him when it hurt.

What a difference! They decided to operate again.

Ellen and Graham looked after Adele when I was being operated on. I had a single room on the eighth floor of the hospital and had a fantastic view over Sheffield. The day before the surgery I was looking out the window and I heard Gilbert come into the room. He threw a box of chocolates on my bed and said "Do you know how much these cost?". The last thing on my mind were chocolates (it's too hot in hospital for chocolate).

I was asked if I was allergic to anything and I told the consultant that I was really sick after every operation I had, so he gave me an injection to stop the sickness. He was happy with the surgery and it was a success. It took me a little while to get back into the swing of things because I hadn't realised how much I used my artificial arm. I discovered that you shouldn't cut bread by holding it with your stump while wearing a dressing gown; you tend to cut slices out of it and I had a very aerated sleeve.

For some time I felt a bit low, so my sister Jenny arranged that we and Adele would go on a little holiday to the seaside. We stayed at Chapel St Leonard's on the east coast. It was a nice enough place, but the first night we had to rush Adele to the A&E department when she had had a very bad asthma attack. She was given some medicine that helped enormously. She didn't want to go home, so we carefully monitored her every movement until we felt confident that she was well enough to stay.

On the other hand, I kept saying to my sister, "I feel odd, but could you please pass that loaf of bread and some butter?" I couldn't stop eating. I couldn't quite put my finger on it, but there was definitely something wrong. After about five months, I went to the doctor, explained my symptoms, and was told that I was pregnant. I remembered the Thalidomide disaster and my first thought was, Oh no, what about that anti-sickness injection I had after my operation? I contacted the hospital but they could not assure me that there would be no problems. My good friend, Ann, in Scotland had a sister who had a Thalidomide baby and I couldn't help thinking about how devastated she was. Also I had a contraceptive coil fitted, so I could not understand how I could get pregnant.

My son Craig was in born December 1980, when Adele was almost nine years old. I had a very bad labour (another thirty six hours), so much so that when Gilbert came into the delivery room he said to me, "What have they done to you?". I thought, I can't be very well, because he would never say anything like that. I looked at my new son with such overwhelming love, knowing that he was sent to keep us all together. He was a long baby and was going to be much taller than Adele. To this day, she insists that Craig got all of her height, as she is five feet two, and he is six feet three. Apart from that, he looked just like her when she was born.

Adele was a great practical help to me. I often look back and smile at the time when Adele was helping me iron some clothes, with her left arm straight down by her side because that's the way I did it. I found it quite difficult to show her how to do it properly but when Jenny came over, she showed her how it should be done. Also when I put on nail varnish, I put the brush in my mouth to apply it, and so when I saw Adele putting nail polish on her doll, with the brush in her mouth, I had to show her the proper way. Gilbert was busy but he also helped with the baby when he could. I still had not pierced Craig with a nappy pin!

Fortunately, a great invention came along, disposable nappies. What a boon.

Chapter 4

I felt that I had not given Jesus much of my time since He came into my life. Gilbert and I were just scraping by, but much happier, so when Craig was about two, I took a cleaning job, which helped a little. The lady I cleaned for, Jane, was a lovely Christian. We met when we first moved to Dronfield. I was registering at the new doctor's surgery, when the doctor said that he knew of a couple whose new baby had been born with one arm; would I possibly contact her to give her some hope? When we met, a friendship was formed that has lasted to this day. Her lovely baby Mary was so beautiful, and she grew up with absolutely no hang ups. She is now a beautiful young lady and it has been a pleasure to know her and her family. Jane impressed me so much with her attitude.

My sister Ellen and her husband Graham had both become Christians and I knew that they all had something I did not have. One day Jane said to me, 'I have been told by the Lord to tell you that you should go to church, so I will take you next Sunday'. She called for me and drove me to a church deep in a housing estate. What an experience! It was something I did not expect, people were laughing – were you allowed to laugh in church? They were obviously enjoying themselves. Jane said to me, 'Next week, you're on your own.' The following Sunday I jumped into the car and drove round for a long time before I could find the church.

Eventually I found it and everyone welcomed me; it was wonderful. They shared the 'peace' together, including me in the proceedings. I felt at home.

After some time, I started to pray more. I always thought that it was not the done thing to pray for help with finances, but I just couldn't see a way out of the situation we were in. So I prayed and asked if He could help us in this difficulty. No more than two days later, Gilbert was given a promotion and his salary was almost doubled. This was indeed a miracle and what a difference it makes when financial troubles disappear. Of course, his salary was still not large and we were never destined to be well off, but without help from the Lord we would always have struggled.

During coffee after a service a lady came up to me and introduced herself as Diane. I felt an instant rapport. She invited me to her house for coffee the next day and that was the start of a very important part of my life. She had recently become a Christian and so we were both on the same road of learning. We met every Tuesday afternoon, then Wednesday and Thursday and so on, until we were meeting four times a week. We never seemed to run out of things to talk about and we prayed for half an hour each time we met. We laughed, talked and felt we had known each other for ever.

The church was running a course called 'Saints Alive' and Diane and I went to every meeting. I was a bit overwhelmed by it all, as everything was so unfamiliar. People were talking in a funny way and someone even 'fell down'. I did not know what was going on, but the minister who was leading the course tried to explain that every bad thing I had done in my life had been wiped clean by Jesus dying on the cross. He also said that if I had been the only person alive in the world when He was crucified, He would still have died just for me. This was so enormous that it took quite a while for me to grasp what it meant. After a few weeks I actually prayed out loud and felt such peace afterwards that I knew Jesus was there in my heart.

My sister Ellen and her husband Graham had moved to a beautiful farmhouse in the country. They had two dogs, a lovely cross called 'Bess' and a wonderful huge black and white Newfoundland called 'Wellington', who resembled a small cow. One day Ellen phoned me to say that someone had thrown a little dog from a car on the main road and would I be interested in a dog as she couldn't cope with another? I had always thought about having a dog but with finances the way they were I hadn't thought it possible. However, I went up to see this little scrap of a dog and my heart was taken immediately. We called him 'Max' and he was my dog. Everyone loved him, but he was mine. I didn't know then what part he was to play in my walk, literally, with God.

Billy Graham came to Sheffield in 1985 and information came round the churches that a three-thousand-strong choir was to be formed for the five nights he was there. We had to go to into town for rehearsals and I felt wonderful that I could sing my praises to the Lord. The choir met once a week, led by a lady called Jackie Williams. She was very small woman but she had a huge personality behind her baton. We learned a great many songs and sang our hearts out as we watched with tears in our eyes as thousands of people came to the Lord on those five wonderful evenings. One evening Cliff Richard was there giving his testimony and singing. What an experience!

When the crusade was over, we heard that the choir

that had been formed would carry on and if anyone wanted to join, please come, as so many people had remarked how wonderful the large choir was. Around five hundred people turned up and the Mission Sheffield Choir was born. After a few years the name was changed to the Celebration Choir. We met in a Baptist Church in town every Thursday. No auditions were held, we were just asked to sit in sections for the parts we thought were right for our voices. After I few times changing places, Diane and I were ensconced in the descant soprano section. We were up in the balcony of the church, surrounded by three other choir parts. After a few weeks of studying the music and loving everything we were singing, we had a fit of the giggles for some reason or other. We were being watched by some people who were looking disapprovingly at us, which made it even harder to stop. These were the sort or rehearsals we had for many years.

We sung at a concert in Sheffield City Hall, which was very exciting. The last choir I had sung in was at school, many moons before, so I thought to myself, I hope I'll be standing behind someone very tall, but I was just so happy singing in a choir with a huge sound. After the concert we couldn't wait for the next rehearsal.

At about this time I had been feeling very unwell and terribly tired with no energy. I went to the doctor and told him that I had been bleeding every day for about a year. I was told that I had to have a hysterectomy – another trip to hospital. I felt relieved, even though it was not a pleasant thing to have done. Diane was distraught and prayed for me constantly, hoping that I wouldn't have to have the surgery. It went ahead and after a few weeks' recovery, my life was so much better. I'm afraid that I never once thought that I was no longer a 'proper woman', I was just so thankful to be feeling well.

I had to give up my cleaning job as I was having trouble with my elbow. I went to the doctor again and was told I had tennis elbow. Good grief! The last time I lifted a tennis racket, I was fifteen. I was told to rest my arm but found that was totally impossible. Even lifting the kettle was a struggle. Why is it that a pint of milk contains at least a gallon when dropped? And I dropped many a pint of milk. I was prescribed course of cortisone injections, which seemed to help at first but the effects wore off very quickly. I had three more courses before succumbing to the surgeon's knife again. I'm pleased to say that the operation was a complete success.

Diane was upset as she had arranged to go on holiday with her family for two weeks, just as I was due for surgery. She said she would not telephone me from France as I would not be able to lift the phone, so she wrote to me every other day.

On her return from holiday, Diane found out that there was a church that held healing services and she wanted to take me so that I could recover more quickly from the discomfort I was feeling. It was a fair way out of town but we went along with our friend Val. On arriving at the church, several nuns were coming out and my old upbringing came flashing to my mind, thinking how my parents would frown on me if they could see me now. As we sat down and prepared for the service, I was totally overwhelmed by the singing that suddenly burst forth from nowhere, in incredible harmony. I closed my eyes and was lifted to a place I had never been before. I learned later that people were 'singing in tongues', something I had only heard about in our meetings. I have never heard anything

81

as sublime since that time, a little taste of Heaven.

Diane and I had a relationship that was completely different from any other that I had known. We knew what each other was going to say, we thought the same thoughts, and even when I was vacuuming the carpet I knew when the she was going to phone me, so I would switch it off just in time to hear the phone ringing. She was very down-to-earth and every person she met knew she was a Christian. She did not 'Bible Bash' at them, but just the way she treated people and the attitude she had, showed everyone how thoughtful and kind she was. At her place of work she asked her colleagues not to swear in front of her and their reaction was one of respect. I greatly admired her for that, as I don't think I would have done the same, much to my shame of course.

Since I had to give up my cleaning job, I felt I had to do something with my time which didn't involve actually doing anything, a good trick! I decided to volunteer in a hospice and was sent to the Occupational Therapy Department. The people there were day patients, brought in by car once a week to have their hair done, medicine checked and just to chat with each other. I had a wonderful time. There was music playing and I would sing along and they would join in, and every Monday we looked forward to a sing song. The men and the ladies who were able, danced, and it was a very happy place. I managed to help with basket making, baking and crafts, and got to know many of the patients very well.

There was a tiny little lady who was one of my favourites. I know you shouldn't have favourites but she was so sweet, and what a life story! She had been married and had six children, then her husband died tragically when her youngest was only eighteen months old. Two years later she met and married a widower who had seven children. Thirteen children! I haven't a clue how she managed.

I also loved talking to the men who shared their stories of the war with me. There was a chap called Frank from Ireland, who told me that he had escaped from a camp in Burma and walked for about three months before being picked up by the Allies, by which time he weighed only seven stones. I have always been fascinated by the individual stories that these brave men would share with me, yet they were so blasé about them.

We were still attending the choir every second week and one night Jackie Williams said that she was going to put on a concert called 'Triumph in the Church'. She was looking for soloists and asked volunteers to put their names on the list at the front before leaving. Diane looked at me and then she frog-marched me to the door and said "Put your name on that piece of paper". So I did. I knew that I would not be called back for an audition because I did have not the confidence to sing solo, except in the shower. The concert was to be held in the Sheffield City Hall, so there was a little part of me that hoped that I wouldn't be chosen, but on the other hand I would love to do it.

I was sitting watching TV one Saturday night when the phone rang and I was astounded to hear Jackie Williams asking if I would come for an audition; I answered in a high pitched voice, of course. Diane drove me to the auditions (I still couldn't drive because of my elbow). There were about thirty people in the hall, all with a piece of music for the pianist to play. I had no music because I was going to sing unaccompanied - Good grief! No pressure then! I sang 'An Eriskay Love Lilt', which I had sung many years before in school. I thought that by singing something unaccompanied, they might not notice if I go flat. I got through it and skulked away to my chair.

I was sitting beside a girl who said her name was Anne. She was just as nervous as me and we consoled each other, sharing our Polo Mints. I was to meet up with Anne some time later in church and we have remained friends ever since. I'm afraid that she and I were terrible gigglers when rehearsing for the choir. Some of our fellow singers would look over their specs at us with some withering glances, which of course made it ever harder to stop. Laughing is such a tonic and I'm sure Anne and I are fully topped up with a good dose of Complan.

One night I got a phone call again from Jackie to say that I had been chosen to sing a solo in the concert. I have never been on such a good diet, as I lost around five pounds in the next week. We met again and I had to sing two songs to see which one suited my voice. The song chosen for me was 'Lord Have Mercy'. I prayed many times that the Lord would have mercy on me and help me get through the ordeal. We were doing three nights in the City Hall and rehearsals were frantic. Diane was so pleased for me and told everyone what was happening, although I did try to tell her that I preferred a low profile.

The day of the first concert arrived and I was terrified. My friends were all praying for me but I could not seem to get rid of the lump in my throat. I was sitting with the other descants at the top of the staging and when the time came for me to sing, I had to walk down many flights of stairs, go under the stage and come up at the other side. On my way there I was hoping I would not get lost and come up through a door in the middle of the audience.

I waited at the side of the stage and prayed hard that Jesus would be there to help me. I heard my cue, walked on and I felt my hand burning as if someone was holding it. I looked up at the circle, into the spotlight that was shining on me, and I saw Jesus. I felt calm and elated at the same time, knowing that I was doing this for Him not for me. The song was well received and I couldn't sleep that night thinking of all the wonderful things that had happened to me. The next two nights were similar and I felt Jesus so close to me.

Diane and I had started to attend a church in Sheffield that had the most wonderful vicar. We had sermons that lasted about forty-five minutes, but seemed like only ten. We met Anne, the lady with whom I had auditioned for the concert, and it was the start of another wonderful friendship. Diane had decided to go on a Lay Readers course, which would take three years. She was holding Bible meetings in her house every Monday night and she thought she would benefit from such a course. She enrolled in 1990 but a few weeks into her course she told me that she a found a small lump in her breast. I said immediately "Please go to the doctor", but I think she waited a little while before making an appointment.

I went with her to the consultant, who told her that she had cancer. She worked in a bank and had joined a health scheme and so her surgery was organised very quickly. She had a complete mastectomy, but was very calm about it, much more so than I was. She had to go through radiotherapy every day for several weeks and this took its toll on her. She suffered a sort of sunburn and was very uncomfortable, but she smiled all the way through her ordeal. She was in hospital for a week and it was the only time she missed an appointment on her Lay Readers course.

Our friendship grew stronger than I thought possible. Diane wanted to do lots of things she hadn't done, so we would go out for coffee, to the Theatre, and walking with my little dog. She went with family on camping holidays, which they all enjoyed so much, and sent me lots of postcards. She had a great gift for verse and wrote to me in poems, telling me that our friendship was so special and that God was good for bringing us together.

At this time, Diane and I met a young lady, Alison, from Wales, who had moved to Dronfield and was attending our Church. She lived only a few hundred yards from my home and I would visit her as often as I could. She had a very good alto voice and we would sing old hymns and harmonise, and just have a good time. I used to come from visiting her with asthma from laughing too much. That's the only time I didn't mind having that problem, because you can't laugh too much. Alison could play the guitar and I always enjoyed going to visit, as I loved to sing along to someone playing the guitar. We are still good friends and have the sort of friendship where, even if we don't see each other very often, it always feels like we met just the day before.

During her Lay Readers course, Diane was asked to lead a short service in Lodge Moor Hospital in Sheffield. I was asked to come along and lead the singing. It was in a small group and I wasn't quite as nervous, so I thoroughly enjoyed our many times at Lodge Moor. On one occasion there was no one to play the organ for us but Diane knew of a lady who went the church who played the piano and we asked her to come along and help us. The lady was called Sylvia, and she brought her own keyboard and helped us out more than once. Sylvia was to play a great part in my life, although I didn't know it then.

As the years went on I noticed that Diane was suffering more and more pain, but she did not complain once. However, she told me that I was not to pray for healing for her. I did not know why she would ask me that, as I wanted her healing more than anything. I felt I was in a very awkward position as I wanted to pray for healing for my friend but she did not want that: if I prayed for healing, I was betraying her. What was I to do?

In 1993, she was told that the pain in her hip was sciatica and was given pain killers, which did not help at all. She went of her own volition to a physiotherapist, hoping that he would be able to give her some exercises to alleviate the pain, but after one session he more-or-less told her that it was no good and that he could do nothing for her. In the summer of 1993, Diane and her husband went camping in Ireland. I could not imagine how she managed camping in her condition, but I know she enjoyed the wonderful scenery. When she came back, she brought me a cassette of Irish Folk music. I don't think she really knew how much I loved Folk Music and I played it over and over, already knowing most of the songs on the tape and loving every one of them.

A really strange thing happened to me a few weeks later when I was walking the dog over the lovely fields we have near us. The music from the tape was going round and round in my head in a way that had never happened before. Then different words came to me which fitted in with the music and before I knew it, I had three verses of a Christian song. I wondered what Max must thought was going on, as he kept looking round at me to see who I was talking to. I couldn't wait to tell Diane. I saw her that afternoon and told her immediately what had happened. She asked me to sing it to her. The words were exactly my testimony:

My spirits were low, and my life in despair,
My heart it was broken and no one did care,
And the things that I did brought no happiness there
And darkness it seemed to surround me.
Then I heard Jesus' voice as it called out to me,
'Lay all your fears on me and I'll set you free
And I will love you throughout eternity'.
I reached out my hand and He held me.
The darkness it lifted, His light blazed on through
In that precious moment my life was brand new,
And the sins in my life He forgave me I knew.
When I gave my life to Lord Jesus,
I was loved in a way as never before,
And with gladness in my heart I opened the door
And I knelt at the feet of my dear Lord in Awe.
He reached out His hand and I held Him.
So look to the cross of our dear risen Lord,
The cross that was stained by His precious life's blood
That was shed for mankind in one great act of love.
That we'd kneel at His throne, pure, before Him,
The King of creation is willing to give
The water of life, so drink deeply and live.
And be sure in your heart that you'll share in the gift
Of the love in the life of Lord Jesus.

For the next few weeks, every time I took Max over the fields a new song came to me. I couldn't believe that Jesus was talking to me and yet I heard Him. I felt privileged that I had been chosen for something so special. What was I going to do with these songs? I hadn't a clue, but I felt I had been given them for a reason. I had composed fourteen songs. Diane listened to every one and with each one she was more excited and more complimentary.

She was now feeling very ill and I knew she wasn't telling me the exact truth of how she really was. She told me later that she was trying to spare my feelings. I'm not sure if this worked out the way she'd hoped, because as the ever-eternal optimist, I still hoped – as I couldn't pray – that she would be healed. She was told that she had bone cancer that had spread throughout her body, so the prognosis was dire. Her consultant told her that her spine was crumbling and that, if she didn't want to be in a wheelchair, she would need surgery to put two steel rods on either side of her spine to strengthen it. She actually did have to use a wheelchair to take her into town and the like, but she struggled on without complaint.

I found it very difficult to push the wheelchair and once, when I was pushing her to our friend Val's house for Bible Study, I suddenly heard a click and my back went out. I couldn't move. I now know what genuine back pain sufferers mean when they say they are in pain; I can really empathise. I had to be carried home and I could not get out of bed the next day. My sister quickly made an appointment with an osteopath. I was helped on to his couch and he said, "Just hold me round my waist and listen", and with two clicks, my back was put back in place. I felt that if I sneezed, something would drop off and it took at least three weeks before it was back to normal. Diane felt awful, believing that she had caused it all, and was inconsolable that she had caused me pain. I tried to tell her that a bad back was nothing compared to her own suffering, but to no avail.

Her surgery was scheduled for April 1994 and she went to hospital full of hope, thinking that she would be up and about in no time. I visited her on the evening of her operation and although she was groggy, she showed me that she could move her toes. Her husband and I left, feeling more elated than we thought possible. I saw her every day and we laughed, joked and talked so loudly that the nurses had to come and close the door (she was in a private hospital). However, on my daily visits I noticed that she was acting very strangely. She wrote letters to all the friends she hadn't seen for some time and asked if I would deliver them. There was one in particular that must have taken her hours to write. Diane could hardly get it into the envelope and I struggled to get it through the letterbox; in fact, it was so difficult that the letter box snapped back and almost took the nail off my middle finger – that was a mite painful! Of course I didn't mention it to her but she saw that the end of my finger looked like something from a Tom and Jerry cartoon. She was so upset that she had caused me more pain.

Her husband and I were in church one Sunday evening, a huge church with at least five hundred people there, when a beeper went off and someone stood up and left. We all looked around to see what was happening and then carried on with the rest of the service. Her husband and I went straight to the hospital after church and we learned that the person who was called for during the service had actually been summoned for Diane, who was gravely ill. We went in to see her and she was semi-conscious, not knowing we were there. The last thing I heard her say through her dream-like state was the Lord's Prayer. Even then she was thinking of Jesus.

I was driven home and went to bed in a very sad state. Of course I couldn't sleep and at five o'clock the next morning I got a phone call from Diane's husband to say that she had gone, and asking if I would like to come to say goodbye. He collected me and an hour later I said my last goodbye to my very special friend. I went home with a heart so heavy that I couldn't cry. It was the 18th of April on a beautiful morning and I had to take Max for his walk. I couldn't believe that the world hadn't stopped. Here I was, looking at the glorious sun shining on all the lovely hills that are so wonderful in the Peak District that Diane and her family loved so well. How could I carry on without her? Where would I ever find such a wonderful friend? After walking the dog, I cried and couldn't stop.

Diane had always asked that when she was gone, I should carry on going to church with her husband Terry, and for a long time afterwards we went together. She also hinted to me that I should start going to a church that was in my parish, rather than travelling to another part of Sheffield. I asked the vicar's wife what she thought and she said that I should try to find a lively Baptist Church in my area, and so I did. On the first Sunday at the new church I walked in and saw at least ten people from the Celebration Choir. I felt I had come home and settled in there so easily that I have been there ever since.

During her illness, Diane's son, Stephen, and his lovely partner Kate, bought a beautiful house. Terry and Stephen were quite a team in the DIY department, so most weekends they were out renovating. I was invited to their wedding and was asked to sing. It was so difficult to do, as there was an empty place – not literally – where my friend should have been. Over the years the house has been changed into the most handsome home for Stephen, Kate and their two lovely boys, Joshua and Henry. I was visiting them recently and Henry came and sat on my knee to ask if I was his Grandma. With tears in my eyes I tried to explain that I was not his Grandma but I was her best friend and that she would have loved them very much and would have been very proud of them.

I still was volunteering in the Hospice, where everyone was so kind to me because they knew how Diane's death had affected me. One Christmas I was asked to sing a few songs at the department's party and they were received quite well. People had been asking me why had not been doing it for longer. If they only knew how hard I have to pray before I sing. It sounds strange, but when I sing for Jesus I am terribly nervous. I have never understood why; maybe it's because I try so hard to sing my best and sometimes I think that I fail miserably. I don't seem to be nearly as nervous when singing secular songs; it's most peculiar.

My sister Jenny, who lived just round the corner from me, asked if we could join a club or something, so we went to the Townswomen's Guild and enjoyed many of their meetings. We were looking forward to the Guild's Christmas Dinner in a local hotel, and talked about what we would wear. At this time I was still wearing my prosthetic arm, which had a new latex hand, but unfortunately it was very difficult to keep clean. I had been wearing a glove on it, but because I left my hand all over the place and was sometimes late for appointments because I couldn't find 'the bloomin' thing', the glove was in constant need of washing. Taking the glove off was rather easier that putting it on, because the latex would stick against any material it came into contact with. So I had a brainwave – I would wash the glove without taking it off the hand.

I did this and it came up a treat, but unfortunately I didn't dry it properly on the evening of the Christmas party. We were all having a lovely time and enjoying the banter and the wonderful food. As the evening drew to a close and people stood up to leave, I noticed that the lady I had been sitting next to had a huge dark patch on her royal blue dress and she was wondering how it could have happened. I was very naughty and did not own up to the fact that it was my 'brainwave' that had been leaning against her and had left a great damp patch on her lovely frock. I always felt a little sheepish afterwards when attending the meetings.

Another incident involving my 'rogue appendage' was one morning when Gilbert and I got up and we noticed that both our cars had been broken into. Gilbert's radio had been stolen, ripped from the car without much finesse, but the only thing that was stolen from my car was my new latex hand, which, I hate to admit, I would leave wherever I took it off, so normally it was on the parcel shelf. I telephoned the police and the local radio station, hoping that someone would own up and return it. About three days later a policeman knocked on my door holding a brown paper bag and asked if it could be mine. I opened the bag and saw that my hand was covered in mud and other unmentionables. The policeman explained that a keen gardener was raking through his compost heap and had discovered my hand. I only hope that he had a strong heart. I took me a long time to clean it properly and it was never the same again. I put in an order for another one as soon as I could.

We continued to go to our friend Val's house for Bible Study, as she had taken over from Diane. Val and Diane met at the same church sometime before we did. They were very sporty and used to play tennis and squash and go swimming. I would have liked to join in, but having to take care of my arm I felt that I should give this a miss. They enjoyed their games and were both very competitive. Sometimes I would go to watch a squash game but I couldn't even see the ball as it whizzed around the court. I'm glad I had an excuse to say "No thank you".

Sylvia started going to the Bible Study and we got to know each other much more. One evening at the Bible Study, Val asked what had happened to all the songs that the Lord had given me. I said, "Absolutely nothing", but it put the idea in my head that I could record them professionally. How on earth do you do that? The Lord has an answer for everything. I had sung at a little folk club in my town and someone from church, whose son was a friend of Craig's, had once said to me "Have you ever thought of going into a recording studio?". He told me that he could do the job for me but I knew, even before asking, that the cost would be prohibitive.

Val said that she would fund it, if I could arrange it. My friend Alison, whom I had known for a few years, could play the guitar but she was looking for someone to teach her further, and so I was told about David, a chap in our church who was an extremely accomplished guitarist. I approached him and he said he would be interested in the project, so we arranged to meet and go through the music. I did not have any music written down, so I sang the songs to David and he wrote down the chords. When he felt confident with the song, he put in the 'twiddly bits'.

We met several times and eventually we contacted the studio and booked it for a few days. David was wonderful and he made the songs sound so meaningful. The producer said that he thought that some of the songs needed additional instrumentation to bring out the melodies and I contacted Sylvia, who immediately offered to help. She brought her keyboard and instantly chose the right sounds and chords. It was quite an experience standing in a sort of black box, surrounded by what looked like black egg boxes, which were for soundproofing. It took three days to complete the recording of the songs, which then had to go back for editing and timing etc. I decided to call the tape, as it was then, 'My Life has been Blessed', as I felt that despite everything that had happened in my life, I could now say that it had been blessed. I was worried about the finances, knowing that a recording studio was going to cost a lot of money, but my dear friend Val did as she promised and paid for everything. I said that if I should sell any, the money would go instantly to her. Val didn't seem to worry about that, having more faith in me than I had.

The producer gave me the names of people who could print labels and tapes, so everything was set to go. The minimum amount we could order was 500 and we imagined that they would spend many years on a shelf, getting dusty. Both my children are extremely gifted artistically and Adele designed the cover for the cassette. It took her a long time as she hand-drew the intricate Celtic knot work that would go around the edge of the cassette. After they were edited, produced and printed, Craig and I sat for many an hour, putting them together. I hadn't thought about who would buy them but Val had an idea about that. She arranged that we would have a 'launch' in our local civic centre. The evening would be dedicated to Diane and all proceeds would go to the MacMillan Nurses.

When I arrived at the hall I was astonished to see so many people. David and Sylvia were there to help me with the music, and I gave my testimony. I could only think of my Dad; would he be proud of me if he could see me now? I had been worried about having to speak for over an hour, but it went more easily than I expected, or feared. I was told that the evening was a great success and it raised over two hundred pounds, which was quite a good amount for that time, and we did not overcharge for the tapes. My songs were well received, as I knew they would be, because they had nothing to do with me but were from God. The title of the collection, 'My Life has been Blessed' is very relevant to my whole story:

My life has been blessed, I love and I'm loved
By the Son of the Father in heaven above
And I'll be rewarded so well for this love
For some day I'll be with Him in heaven
He shone through the dark of my life filled with sin
He gave me what I longed for, His peace deep within
I opened the door when I heard His voice call
From that day I have walked with Lord Jesus
My heart soars on high like a bird on the wing
With Lord Jesus beside me, His praises I'll sing
My life has been filled with His mercy and grace
And love flows through my soul from Lord Jesus

The title of the song jumped at me and in that moment I knew that my life had been blessed, because I could now empathise with the many different trials that people have to endure. What I have gone through seems really trivial.

Another part of my story is that Alison, who asked

David to teach her the guitar, had fallen for him and was so excited that he felt the same. And, lo and behold, sometime later a wedding was being planned and I felt that God's hand had guided so many aspects of my life.

I was still going to the church that Diane and I had attended and where I met my friend Anne. She and I still giggle each time we meet, but one incident happened that we will never forget. At Easter time it was announced that there would be an 'Agape' meal, and we arranged to meet at Church. There were at least a hundred people in the Church Hall and we sat down at a table on which there was fruit, bread and fruit juice. We were sitting opposite a lovely couple who were, can I say, slightly more posh than me. I decided not to have an orange, although I can peel an orange at home with a tea towel on my knee, but there was nothing there that I could use, so Anne and I decided to have a banana. We picked up the banana and proceeded to peel and eat it. But as we were tucking into our fruit, the lovely couple opposite us also took a banana each, peeled it and put it on their plates, cut it up into little slices, sprinkled sugar on it and ate it with a knife and fork. The performance left Anne and me looking slightly sheepish as we ate our fruit like a couple of chimps. I don't think a purple face suited either of us.

One of my fellow volunteers at the Hospice, a lovely lady called Molly, had once said that she belonged to a bowling club and that the entertainers they booked were pretty dire. She asked if my friend Sylvia and I would 'do an hour' for them. We agreed, but when we started rehearsing I began to realise how many songs you can get through in an hour. It was with some trepidation that we arrived at the club's premises, a rather large hall, and set up the keyboard and microphone. We were received very well but as Sylvia and I have said since, we didn't do much chatting in between songs, which we do nowadays because I know people appreciate it. To have a rapport with the audience makes the whole thing much easier. We began to be asked more often to entertain, especially in nursing and residential homes.

There have been many incidents on our journey through 'entertaining' and we have forgotten most of them, but the few I can remember will stick in my mind forever. Before we arrive, Sylvia always phones to confirm the arrangements and asks if there is a piano or if she should bring her keyboard. Once she asked the 'piano question' and they replied that there was one and that it had been tuned. When she sat down later to test it, she found that it had probably been tuned in 1952. There were notes that wouldn't play and every time she pressed the loud pedal it sounded as if there was a Jack Russell hiding among the strings. I found it quite difficult to sing with my hand in my mouth, as every time I sang a certain note, I had a 'bark' as a harmony. When I burst forth with 'All the Nice Girls Love a Sailor', there was a gentleman sitting looking at me up and down through an invisible telescope. Quite disconcerting!

On another occasion we were asked to entertain at a beautiful residential home in the Peak District. It was to be a Forties celebration and we were asked to sing all the old songs of that period. We delved into our stack of music and managed to come up with quite a selection. We decided to sing 'The Quarter Master's Store', in which we like to incorporate the names of some of the residents. We found out some names and made up little rhymes, for instance, 'There was Anne, looking for a man in the stores...'

A gentleman came up and said could we 'do' his name, which was Ken. Well, 'Ken was looking for a Wren', and he was so excited that afterwards he wanted to know her name and address. We tried to explain that it was only a rhyme but we found out later that he had been a bit of a ladies' man when he was in the Navy and he thought the Wren was real. Oh well!

We were at a hall in a very posh part of the town and Sylvia was told that there was a grand piano. She was looking forward to playing it. The top was opened to bring out the lovely tone of the instrument but she couldn't see the audience. I started to sing 'Somewhere Over the Rainbow' and got to the part where it says 'way up high', when a lady on the front row took her teeth out and started to clean them with a nail file. The 'high' came out as 'ha ha ha' and it was even funnier because Sylvia couldn't see what was going on. When I regained consciousness, I managed to finish the song.

We have been asked by the residents to do many medical things for them, which I couldn't possibly relate, and thank goodness we could always say, 'I'll go and get a carer'.

One particularly memorable event happened when singing in the choir in Peterborough. After a concert a lady rushed up to me, grabbed my hand and said "Your voice is so much younger than your face". It's just as well my skin is slightly thicker these days. I think she realised what she had said and tried to back-pedal, but it was too late. The story always amuses me.

During this time we were still singing in the choir and we were told that a production company called Kingsway was making a cassette tape series on famous hymn writers and that the Celebration Choir had been chosen to make one of the recordings. We were to make a tape of Fanny Crosby hymns. We rehearsed for months and re-learned the hymns of our youth; a wonderful experience. I'd forgotten how difficult it is to make a recording when every little mistake in the singing or music is instantly picked up in the recording room. We recorded for three nights in a row and were exhausted, but we couldn't wait to hear the result. When you sing in a choir, you can't actually hear what you sound like, so when the recording came out we were amazed at the wonderful sound we made.

When I sat down and really thought about it, I hadn't actually realised how much my life had changed since singing in the choir. It wasn't that my confidence had been built up because I had been singing solos; it had nothing to do with confidence. I don't know how to describe it but I felt that I was meant to being doing this for ever. At every rehearsal there was a sort of buzz in the air, people were so pleased to see each other and the atmosphere was one of excitement and anticipation, and we left at nine thirty feeling fulfilled and happy.

Sylvia and I were becoming very close friends and I couldn't help thinking that, not long before, I felt I could never have another friend like Diane. Sylvia was and is a wonderful sincere friend. Although she is a fantastic musician, playing the piano for the Celebration Choir, she was always very wary of big events. The choir performed two large concerts each year, mostly in the City Hall and the Octagon, which were rather nerve-racking. Many people asked our Musical Director if we could sing in their churches but she had to turn them down as the choir was too large to fit into small churches. Sometime later it was announced that there was going to be a Travelling Choir. A rota would be drawn up and we would take turns to travel to local churches. Since I was one of the soloists, I was very fortunate to be asked to every concert.

We had a wonderful time and travelled around the country. Our first concert was in Sheffield, naturally, but it was 'just testing the water'. Our next was in Sherringham in Norfolk. We had such fun on the journey there, getting to get to know each other, as in a large choir you tend to know only the people in the same section. In the travelling choir we had time for bonding and lasting friendships. The trip to Norfolk was especially interesting because the coach was misdirected though the very narrow streets and the poor driver had to do a thirty-three-point-turn to get back to where we should have been.

Kingsway asked if we could make another recording, which we were most excited about. It was to be the Sankey Hymns. I was privileged to sing a solo in this recording. How could this be happening? To say that my confidence was being built up is just not true, as I still felt that I was not worthy to do this for God. I sang the opening verse of 'Jesus I Come' and then I was asked to sing along in every verse, which was a great joy for me. I'm sure that those wonderful hymns of my youth are still alive in the memories of everyone who attended a Sunday School in the dim and distant past. We did many recordings for Kingsway and each one was a thrill to do. There was a mixture of old and new songs and the choir seemed to sound better with each recording.

In the meantime, Sylvia and I were still singing and entertaining and enjoying every minute. Each home we visited was different and there were very special people in each one. We have been to so many that both Sylvia and I know which one we would like to be placed in when the time comes.

Radio Two contacted the choir to ask if we could lead the Sunday Service one morning. We were all so excited but my excitement turned to terror when I was asked to sing live on the radio. Some days before the service the producer phoned me to ask what song I was going to sing. I hadn't thought that far ahead but something told me to answer, 'I Reached Out My Hand'. He asked me to sing it down the telephone and all he said was, "That'll do". Singing at eight-thirty in the morning is not easy and all my friends were praying for me. My heart was in my mouth as I walked toward the microphone, thinking, 'Please Lord, let me do this for you'. I was introduced and as soon as I got the first note out, I knew He was there with me. I was very flattered when the producer came up to me and said that I was quite a find – me! He asked if I would be interested in singing on the Daily Service, to which I said "Yes", but unfortunately I never heard from him again. On reflection, the Lord has His plans for us, so that couldn't have been in His plan for me.

Craig, who now about fourteen, came home from school feeling very unwell, sick and with a pain in his stomach. I rushed him to the doctor, who diagnosed appendicitis and immediately phoned the hospital. I phoned Gilbert at work and he said he would go straight to the hospital. I waited in the ward with Craig until it was time for his surgery, but Gilbert had not arrived. I was talking to the nurse at the reception desk when a man came up to me asked if I was Mrs Ritchie. When I said that I was, he rather sheepishly said that he was the driver who had knocked my husband off his motorbike on the way to the hospital.

Trying to be in two places at once is not easy. I stayed with Craig until he was wheeled away, then I rushed to the A&E department to see what state Gilbert was in. Fortunately he was able to stand up and had no major injuries. His arm was badly cut and his finger was broken; so thank God it was not worse. Seeing that he was able to be left on his own, I rushed back to Craig, who had by then been operated on and was a bit groggy, so I rushed back again to Gilbert. We waited several hours until he was patched up and able to go home. He had a great hole in his arm that took many months to heal. I knew he would probably suffer some post-traumatic stress, but being a man, he denied all knowledge of this. I didn't, but found it hard not to say "I told you so" when he did.

We visited Bunty for a few weeks' holiday once or twice a year. She loved the markets, as I don't think there were markets like that in Glasgow at the time. She always travelled back home with her car loaded down with her purchases. When she arrived back home, she would telephone us to say that she had forgotten to buy many more things. She gave us a long list of items to buy and we would take them up to Scotland the next time we went on holiday.

The first time we went on holiday without Adele was quite memorable. We phoned her every night to check that everything was alright and in her normal teenage way she said "Of course I am". After the third night, I thought I would get the usual reply but I was shocked to hear her sobbing on the other end of the phone. She told me that she had slept downstairs the previous night as she had seen a huge spider in her room and she couldn't find it, so had slept on the settee. She had tried to hoover it up but the nozzle was too short for her to get near enough! I will return to this incident later in my story.

Adele had wanted to be a nurse for some time but was having second thoughts. She was an outdoor girl and didn't think she would like to be inside a building every day. So she applied to be a driver for the Patients' Transport in a hospital in Sheffield. She thoroughly enjoyed her time there and brought us many a tale about the lovely elderly people she met. After about eighteen months she saw an advert in the hospital for training as an ambulance technician. She applied and got a post as a technician, passing her training with flying colours. She has since gone on to pass her exams to be a Paramedic and is now training to become part of a Hazard Area Responders Team, the first to attend a terrorist attack, nuclear disaster or chemical spillage. Just when I thought my heart was improving! I must say that both my children have a great love of music, for which I'm really thankful because it has such qualities of soothing, healing and being able to totally consume you in every situation.

I was still being asked to give my testimony in places in and around Sheffield and I was thankful for the opportunity to share my witness with others. Sylvia couldn't always be with me, so I had to sing unaccompanied but it never really bothered me to do so. I was asked to give my testimony at a very large church where I was faced with a huge room-full of people. I talked for about forty-five minutes, in between singing my special songs, and afterwards a beautiful young blonde lady came up to me and asked if I would come to her house as she would love to sing with me. Her name was Mitzy and she was from Nashville Tennessee.

I soon got caught up in the whirl of her enthusiasm,

although I felt that I couldn't possibly match her talent. She had been classically trained and was used to singing Gilbert and Sullivan and the lead roles in famous operas. Having been born in Nashville, she was a great Country and Western fan and wanted to start singing those songs again. With typical dynamism, and before I knew it, she arranged for some musicians to meet and booked a venue for the new 'band'. She called us Celtic Blonde – I was the Celtic she was the blonde. I would sing harmony on every song. I was fortunate in being able to harmonise to most songs; it was something I learned when I was younger, singing with my sisters.

The venue was jam-packed but I was not really nervous, not the way I felt when singing for the Lord. I had a fantastic time and couldn't sleep that night for all the songs going around in my head. Mitzy arranged many more 'gigs' and always included some Christian songs in the programme, which was what I wanted to do all along. The audiences enjoyed our performances and I couldn't wait for the next one. It continued for about two years, with many terrific engagements, but one day Mitzy stopped calling and I never heard from her again. I didn't feel too bad about this, as although I enjoyed singing with her, I felt that I had done God's work for the time He wanted me to.

Chapter 5

During this period Bunty had been having quite a bad time and wanted to move from Glasgow to live near her sons. Keith, Gilbert's brother, and his wife Louise, had moved to a lovely little village in Lincolnshire and they arranged to have her name put down on the local authority housing list. It wasn't too long before she was able to move to a little bungalow about five miles from their house. Her life was much happier and we all felt better that she was nearer. We used to visit as often as we could at weekends, as Gilbert was still working. We phoned each other often; she was always doing competitions in magazines and papers, and when she couldn't get the answer we would work it out together.

Back in Scotland, Gilbert's uncle George became ill and sadly, after just a few weeks, he died suddenly without us saying goodbye. Jean was obviously bereft and we noticed that she also was not looking very well. Some months later we had a phone call from her asking if we would look after Tweetie, since she was going into a nursing home for a month or two. Knowing that Gilbert was very fond of the parrot – I couldn't see the attraction myself – the bird was brought down from Prestwick to Dronfield. Our beloved little Max had been put down a few years before, due to old age, and I think that's why Gilbert was quite keen to have Tweetie. Three months later, Jean phoned to say that she could not take the bird back as she was going to stay in the nursing home. Tweetie was now ours - thanks!

The parrot had the most beautiful cage, made by my very gifted 'DIYer' husband. It looked remarkably like the tenement I used to live in and it completely obscured the patio window, but the parrot and Gilbert were happy. Tweetie was thirty-three years old when we got him. He seemed to bond with the men in his life and would sit beside Gilbert for hours, but one night I was doing a crossword at the dining room table when he suddenly hopped over and showed me that he would like to be scratched round his neck. I obliged, with great trepidation, but from then on he and I were firm friends. We would have whistling competitions, which he always won. We were told that he ate Golden Delicious apples, pistachio nuts, mushrooms and, when they were in season, peas straight from the pod. He cost us a pretty penny over his time with us. We were always amused when watching him eat his apple, taking great chunks, spitting them out and eating the pips. Unfortunately there was nowhere to buy a bag of apple pips.

Bunty was also very fond of Tweetie and offered to look after him if we wanted to go on holiday. My sister and brother-in-law are very adventurous and have been to America several times. They often told us wonderful stories of the places they had seen and it stirred up our enthusiasm so much that they asked us to join them if they went there again. We didn't know what to say, apart from the fact that we would have to take some time to save up for such a trip. But we arranged to do it in a year's time. The only thing I could think of was the flight. It had been many years since I'd been in a plane, but with the help of a kind doctor who supplied four little tablets, two for going and two for coming back, I managed it.

We flew to New York, where we did all the 'touristy' things, including a trip on a ferry boat around Manhattan. I was so overcome when sailing past the Statue of Liberty that I could feel tears in my eyes, thinking of where we were brought up and how far we had come. We stayed for three days in New York then flew to Denver, picked up a huge motor home and set off to explore. We clocked up over three thousand miles travelling around, each sight better than the one before. We visited Las Vegas and the Grand Canyon, and when I saw this spectacle, I knew that God had His hand in the creation of such a wonder. It was so amazing that nobody wanted to speak and when we did it was in whispers; there was a sort of spiritual veil over us and we didn't want to break the magic.

We had a tour around Monument Valley with a driver called Emmerson. He was a native American and he cared a great deal for his land. Although it was not his job, he would collect and dispose of any litter he found. He took us to a sort of cave that had been eroded by the wind to take the shape of a huge eye. Emmerson sang a song in his native tongue and it was extremely moving. Louise asked me to sing and the atmosphere was so moving that we all had the hairs standing up on the backs of our necks.

After being on holiday for three weeks, I couldn't wait to get back to the choir. We had engagements all over the country, some as far away as the Isle of Wight and a wonderfully named place in Scotland called Auchtermuchty. We were getting to know each other in the travelling choir and the fellowship was amazing.

My friend Jane and her husband Robin attended a church that was trying to raise funds to extend their hall.

They decided to have a garden party in the lovely grounds of their beautiful home and they asked if Sylvia and I would entertain their guests. We decided to sing songs from around the world and had great fun selecting those that the audience would sing along with. The day came and the sun was shining as, with the help of a technical whiz kid, we set up the speakers and microphone. I had never sung in the open air before and I was curious to see how we would cope. It all went well until the farmer in the field next door started to burn something. The next thing I knew I was coughing between each verse. Fortunately the evening was coming to an end and I thanked Goodness that the farmer hadn't started his bonfire at the start of the evening (although if I was paranoid enough, I would say that he did not like what I was singing and thought 'I'll sort her'). Despite the coughs, it went well and Jane and Robin immediately asked us if we could return the next year.

Bunty had lived in her little house for about four years when I noticed she was losing weight. She didn't want to talk about it; this was a similar scenario I went through with Diane. I respected her wishes and we continued with our normal conversations. Eventually she went to the doctor who referred her to a consultant who said that she had to have surgery. She was terribly frightened and I couldn't help but think how small and sad she looked, nothing like the lady I first met all those years ago.

The day of her surgery came and we all went to visit her. We could tell by the doctor's demeanour that something was wrong. She was in the intensive care unit, linked up to many machines and tubes. She couldn't speak but we could tell by her eyes that she knew she was dying. The four of us went back to Keith and Louise's house and stayed overnight.

We hadn't gone home to change so I borrowed some clean underwear from Louise. I didn't have a bag to put my used clothes in, so I put my knickers in the pocket of my coat and we went straight back to the hospital.

Bunty managed to squeeze my hand while I told her that everyone who loved her was there with her and she just closed her eyes and drifted peacefully into a coma. The doctor came and said that there was nothing more to be done, and asked for our consent to turn off the machines. I was desperately upset because Bunty and I had shared our thoughts and dreams – we were soulmates. In the midst of my tears, I reached into my coat pocket for a tissue and – guess what – found myself drying my tears with my underwear. Unfortunately we all burst out laughing, I think because of our grief, and had to rush away very quickly before the nurses had time to call the porters to have us evicted for being so ghoulish!

The funeral service was held in the village where Bunty lived before moving to Lincolnshire. She was buried alongside her husband, Gilbert, in a beautiful cemetery overlooking the Solway Firth. We visit them as often as we can when visiting family in Glasgow. When we had the sad task of clearing her house, we found the most wonderful treasures including dresses, or frocks as she used to call them, from the 1930s, some of them covered in finely coloured bugle beads. We also found a receipt for a 'petticoat' from 1957 which cost 15s 11d in 'old money'. She had boxes of seamed stockings and kid gloves with beautiful little buttons on the wrist. Hats, bags, scarves and lots of costume jewellery were laid out on Bunty's bed and we recalled our fond memories of her. There were love letters from her husband, which we just couldn't open, but also some intriguing postcards sent by Gilbert to Bunty from Berlin and Paris. They were dated at the beginning of 1939, so we now had him down as a spy. I'd like to think that he might have been.

My next encounter with the NHS was because I had always been rather top heavy; as Terry Wogan would say, I had a large 'bozoom'. I had been suffering from bad shoulder pain and back ache and was being treated for constant headaches. I went to the doctor again, who agreed to refer me to a consultant in breast reduction procedures. Although I had wanted the operation for a long time, when the day came I thought, what on earth am I doing here?

After the operation I felt very strange and every time I fell asleep I had the most appalling nightmares, convinced that one of the nurses was trying to smother me with a pillow. During the night a young lady was brought in suffering from shortness of breath. She was in her gym gear and looked extremely fit, but as soon as she was settled the consultant came to see her. It was very quiet – well as quiet as a hospital can get during the night – and we could overhear their conversation. She was asked if she smoked, to which she answered "Yes", so the doctor said that she should stop, as it was obviously not doing her any good, even although she had just come from the gym. As soon as he left, she got up, took her cigarettes out of her bag, put one in her mouth, donned her coat and stormed out.

Unfortunately my bed was right next to the nurses' station and as I was afraid to fall asleep, I quickly became acquainted with their social lives and where they were going on holiday. Why is it that the only thing you want to do in hospital is sleep, but it's so noisy that you can't? At about two o'clock in the morning, a doctor came to my bed to check my progress and he was not very happy with what he found. He called someone and before I knew it, I was wheeled down to the operating theatre and had further surgery. When I came round again I was wrapped up in a type of Baco Foil blanket and was absolutely boiling hot. So, more nightmares to come then.

I was in hospital for six days. Although I felt much lighter, I was rather disappointed that I wasn't as small as I hoped, but the doctors told me it was the best they could do. Everything was fine afterwards. The headaches, back pain and shoulder pain disappeared after a few weeks. At first I couldn't put my arm on when getting dressed but I got used to that and I have never put it on since; what liberation! I now drive an automatic car and can do absolutely everything that I could do before. Again everything that happened seemed to have a plus side. My great ambition was that after surgery I would wear a red satin bra, but I've never followed that one through, even although it would have been nice to see it hanging on the washing line.

Ellen and Graham's house was very large and when Mum and Dad's Golden Wedding anniversary arrived, they arranged for a surprise party for them. All the relatives were invited and told 'not to blab'. Ellen is a wonderful hostess and has the ability to cater for lots of people, something that frightens me to death, so the party was left in her capable hands. With many clandestine meetings and talks, the party was arranged. Lots of people were secreted in an upstairs games room, where the tables were beautifully set. We had to make some excuse to persuade Mum and Dad that they had to come up to the games room to 'see something'. Their faces were a picture which will stay with us for ever. They couldn't believe it; even Uncle Tommy had travelled down from Glasgow, and he had never even been out of Scotland before.

Ellen and Graham asked Mum and Dad to their house to look after their animals, which included geese and chickens. Having come from a tenement, I think they must have found it a bit daunting but they looked after them and had many an altercation with both species. They always had a funny story to tell their relatives and we have some fantastic photos of them in hats, coats and wellies – how glamorous! One particularly amusing picture shows Dad looking like a little devil with his pitchfork.

Mum and Dad visited us quite regularly and we noticed that his health was failing. Mum phoned to tell us that Dad had been taken into hospital in Glasgow, with a very bad chest infection. Mum had said for some time that he was getting very unsteady on his feet and was falling down at lot, which was very difficult for Mum, as he was a large man and she, very small. When the infection had cleared up, the doctors noticed that he was very unsteady on his feet and they decided to put him in a nursing home.

He hated every day he was there and always blamed Mum for deserting him. She visited him every day, even although she had to take two buses there and two back. She never missed, but each day he would make her feel more guilty for leaving him. He was in several homes over the next five years, the last being a short distance from Mum's house. This made her life a little bit easier but although it was out of the question that she would take even one day's rest, she was soon exhausted with the daily visits.

Mum was told that Dad had MRSA and because he was so weak they didn't hold out much hope. She sat with him through the night. His breathing became so laboured that she was trying to breathe for him. Early in the morning she went to the bathroom to wash her face and on her return to his room it was eerily quiet. She was distraught, as she was only away for a few minutes and he was gone. A nurse tried to comfort her by saying that he was only hanging on for her while she was beside him, so when she left the room he just slipped away. She told me recently that he never told her that he loved her until just before he died. He also said he was sorry for the way he treated her for all their married life. There is a line of a song I heard somewhere that says, 'In life I loved you too little, in death I loved you too well'. If only he could have told her this when they first married, both their lives would have been so different.

Mum told me that Dad was very proud of me for making a CD, but he never told me himself; he couldn't convey what he really felt. I hope that I've learned from this experience.

Sylvia and I were entertaining more and more, and I thought that, even at my great age, I would like to have singing lessons, so I asked another soloist in the choir for the name of her teacher. It was a lovely lady called Olive and I have had a wonderful friendship with her ever since. She taught me how to sing, how to breathe, how to stand and act the songs I was singing. She had been an operatic singer in her younger days and had sung in all the famous theatres around England. She instantly recognised my lack of confidence and tried to help, but still I never learned.

I wanted to make another recording, redoing some of the original songs the Lord had given me. I approached Sylvia, who was all for the idea. I also mentioned it to a friend in the choir, which led to one of the Committee members telling me that she knew someone who would sponsor the recording. I was thrilled and we met to discuss what songs would be suitable for the disc. The wonderful thing about this project was that the choir would be singing too. The producer who had managed all the choir's recording was asked to produce the CD.

It was arranged that we would sing over three nights in our local church. My friend, David, who had played on the cassette I had done some years before was asked to accompany us. The musicians from the choir also were asked and I felt privileged to have this tremendous choral sound backing me. The day arrived and with it came my nerves again. The producer was extremely professional and frightened the living daylights out of me. He could hear absolutely everything in his recording booth, coughs, sneezes, coins jingling in pockets. I stood to attention most of the time. After three nights, the recording was finished and then I had to go to his studio in Wakefield for the next five days for editing. That involved listening to every track over and over again. I could hear every flaw but fortunately he could delete anything that wasn't right and tweak any flat notes with the turn of a knob. I wanted to have one fitted to the side of my neck. As I got to know him a little better he became slightly less intimidating. He is a very accomplished musician and has composed music for advertisements and incidental music for American shows.

The cover was designed and printed by other experts and all I had to do was wait for the finished article. It was to be released in December and I couldn't wait. We had a big choir meeting as a Christmas event, and the CDs were delivered. Everyone was so kind, asking me to sign the discs. I did not find out how many were sold and I didn't like to ask as they were not mine, but belonged to whoever had sponsored them. The CD was called 'Lord You Have My Heart'. I listened to it twice and then put it away, as I can't bear to hear myself sign. Am I too much of a perfectionist? Maybe that's not the right word.

When I reached 50, I was contacted by the NHS to go for a mammogram. Many ladies will know how uncomfortable this is, but also that it is very necessary. A few weeks later the dreaded letter came, asking me to go for further tests. I was naturally petrified but I had to go. On arriving for my appointment I kept seeing a rather large chap wearing trainers and a brightly checked shirt. He hurried from one room to another and I thought he was the electrician. When I was called in to see the consultant, it was the 'electrician'!

He showed me the little white dots on the X-ray and said he had to do a biopsy. I sat in a large chair and was told that I would hear a few 'clicks' but would feel no pain. After hearing the clicks, I said "Sorry, I'm going to faint", to which he replied, "Oh no you're not!". But I won - Oh yes I did! I woke up on a trolley, asking if I had to go through that all again and was told that the procedure had been done while I was unconscious. When I returned for the follow up appointment, I was given the all clear; the little dots were calcification of the scars from the breast reduction operation. I felt so lucky, as I saw the other ladies sitting there who did not have such good news.

When we had Max I used to go wandering over the fields and would meet many people doing the same thing. You get to know lots of people when dog walking. I always passed a house with a large hedge that I couldn't see over, but I was always singing or whistling, and one day I heard a voice singing the next line of the song. So began my acquaintance with a lovely retired couple. During the summer months we spoke almost every day and I looked forward to our bit of repartee each side of the hedge. I hadn't seen them during the winter but that was the norm over the cold months. Then I met the lady of the house in the supermarket, who told me that her husband was very ill and that there wasn't much hope. I met her later when she told me that he had died. This is significant in my next encounter with the NHS.

I got a phone call from the lady about a year after her husband had passed away. She was clearly still distressed, so I invited her over for a coffee and a chat. When she arrived, I put the kettle on, but within minutes I felt a sudden pain in my chest which just wouldn't go away. Poor Ethel, I had invited her over for a chat and to talk about her husband, and suddenly she was looking after me. As volunteer in the hospice, I learned that when talking to a recently bereaved person the subject they are most likely to want to talk about is their late partner, but that's probably the subject that most people would avoid. Normally, on approaching the subject of their loved one, the flood gates open. So I was all geared up to help Ethel, but as the pain in my chest wouldn't go, she phoned my sister Jenny, who lives just around the corner from us, who came running over.

She took one look at me and phoned for an ambulance, and I was whipped off to hospital. After some hours, the doctor came to tell me that I had had a heart attack. Why? I was just sitting and talking, but there is a history heart disease in my family and I was the next one to have it. I was in hospital for six days. I just had to lie there and was told not to go walking about. There is only so much television that you can concentrate on in hospital, so I was so glad to get home.

I arrived home just a week before Christmas. Craig had to put up the tree and all the trimmings. Christmas dinner was a bit of a muddle but I was just so glad to be home that I could have been eating porridge and chips and would have been just as delighted – well maybe.

When Gilbert went back to work after the holidays, I found that I didn't want to be left alone. It was something that I had previously enjoyed but my friends kept phoning me. Unfortunately I could hardly get my breath, so my favourite pastime, talking, was cut short. I slowly got my confidence back and felt back to normal when I could go into town on my own.

I thought I was safe from further encounters with the NHS, but it was not to be. I prided myself on going into town on my own, but one day I tripped over a raised flagstone as I stepped off the bus. I came crashing down on my stump and I couldn't move. A gentleman came running out of a shop and he called an ambulance. I just wanted to get up and walk away, but I couldn't. I was taken to a hospital on the other side of Sheffield. On my way there, the paramedics told me to stop talking and to take big breaths of a gas called Entenox. I was saying that Adele was a paramedic and I was probably rambling a bit until they told me again "Be quiet and take big breaths". The gas was extremely powerful and I was soon trying to tell them that although I had lived through the Sixties, I had never smoked anything 'funny' – but I was sure that this gas would have had the same effect. I kept sliding down and saying "Wow!". I hoped they would let me take a little canister home with me, but no. On arrival at the hospital the consultant said that they hoped I hadn't broken any bones in my stump because they didn't know what they would do if I had!

An event in our lives came to make us realize how much the world has changed from our childhood. Craig was still at college when he told us that his girlfriend was pregnant. I'm afraid that my old upbringing came to the fore and all I could think about was his education. However, as with all things that seem insurmountable at the time, it worked out wonderfully and we are now the grandparents of a gorgeous boy called Taylor, who is tall like his dad and has lovely blue eyes. His mum has done a fantastic job of bringing him up, and now he is a bit older, he is showing signs of being a gifted artist, like his dad.

Jenny and I booked tickets to see Barbara Dixon in the City Hall. It was a fantastic show and we were so excited on the way home it was all we could talk about. On arriving home, I was met by a very distressed Gilbert who said that he had suddenly gone blind in his left eye. I phoned NHS Direct and was told that he should take two Paracetamol and make an appointment with the doctor in the morning. I didn't accept this and I drove Gilbert straight to the A&E where he was seen as a priority case. His blood pressure was dangerously high. We were sent to the eye department of another hospital where they found that his retina was almost detached and a blood vessel had burst behind his eye. I think this was one of the most frightening things we had been through together.

Our choir went to the Isle of Wight three months after my heart attack. The coach trip was very amusing as I was told to speak only for three minutes at a time. My friend Jean from the descants had her watch on me and said, "Now be quiet, for the next thirty minutes"; that was extremely hard. We had a wonderful time on the island. The place was beautiful, the weather was fantastic and the concerts were tremendous. We got to know each other well and had endless fun. We had concert dates for the choir for the next eighteen months and we looked forward to each one of them.

I had managed to steer clear of hospitals for a while, but suddenly I felt my shoulder giving me a lot of pain, especially when I tried to lift things from a cupboard. I was sent for physiotherapy and was given a large rubber band thing that I had to tie to the handle of a door and try to build up the muscles around my shoulder by pulling it up and down. This didn't seem to do anything for me apart from giving me a black eye when I let go. I also was sent for acupuncture, which had no effect, and pain killers just didn't seem to work. Apart from making me groggy, they made me sound like Louis Armstrong. I was also given some morphine patches, which had me talking utter nonsense and walking around in a state of being flummoxed with everything. It was another year before I was sent to the hospital and booked in for more surgery. I asked the consultant if I could be fitted with zips and Velcro for easier access next time.

I missed only about three concerts in all the time I was in the choir, so the Lord was very good to me when my surgery was booked for 29th December. Imagine a Scot being in hospital on Hogmanay! Why is it that you seem to go through a procedure that you don't really want to happen in a sort of dream? Gilbert dropped me off and I didn't want him to wait, knowing it would make me more nervous. I was taken to the waiting room, with my stomach down at my toes and waited for the trolley to come for me.

I woke up with a strange, huge blue sling wrapped around my arm from shoulder to wrist. I couldn't sit up, move about, or even get out of bed without doing a sort of limbo movement. I had to be fed by the nurses, which was a very good diet regime as I kept slipping down the bed and my pudding would land on the blue sling thing. I've always had the highest opinion of the health service; practically everyone I've met there has been extremely kind and helpful. Unfortunately this was not the case this time. A lady, dressed all in purple (I felt I should have curtsied), came up to my bed and asked if there was anything I might need help with when I got home. I told her that my husband worked and left home at 6.30 a.m. and did not come back until 5.30 p.m. My son was also working so wouldn't be at home either, so some help would be needed, please. She said that since I had people at home, no help would be available. I tried to explain that I couldn't even wash my face or go to the bathroom without help, but to no avail. I was sent home with a thing that looks like tongs on a stick to enable me to pick things up.

Jenny was upset at my treatment and contacted my doctor. Ten minutes later I was contacted by a very nice lady who said they would arrange for a helper to visit me three times a day. I subsequently got a phone call from the lady in purple, who was equally incensed and complained bitterly that my sister had gone over her head. Thank Goodness that was over. I had to do exercises every day, which meant that the sling contraption had to be taken off and it was very like the Krypton Factor trying to get the bloomin' thing on again.

Through all these little setbacks, I always felt that Jesus was right beside me, helping me to cope with everything.

How else could I have managed? Both my sisters were wonderful to me through this time, Jenny coming over to help with physio and Ellen making our meals.

My ninety-year-old mum decided to come down from Glasgow to look after her 'wean'. It was lovely to have someone at home with me. If I felt like lying down for a while, I could, knowing she would answer the door or the phone.

Sylvia was always concerned and visited me often, bringing smoothies and tasty things to build me up. It was wonderful to know that people were praying for me. The ladies in my church were especially kind, setting up a rota system to make meals for us; so for six weeks, three meals a week were delivered to our house. I have been so lucky in the friends I have and I feel overwhelmed by their love and sincerity.

I recovered quite quickly but was unable to do the things I wanted to. I also lost a lot of weight, which was wonderful and the complete opposite of what I thought would happen, probably because I couldn't reach the biscuit box. I had to work up to going out by myself, as I had a very great fear of falling and which remained with me till some time later.

Jesus was is in my life then and He is still there. I don't think I could have got through many of the knocks without Him. The privilege of having Him in my life has been something I couldn't possibly have imagined. I was glad that He was there as I had to lean on him again. Craig, Gilbert and I went into town one Saturday and while walking outside John Lewis, I tripped over absolutely nothing and, since the normal instinct is to put your arms out, I fell and landed on my stump again. I almost fainted when lying on the ground. It wouldn't stop bleeding and after two hours, Gilbert took me to the good old A&E, where I was X-rayed. They found that a little bit of bone had chipped off the end, so I was patched up again and sent home. My fear of falling was even more extreme now. When people in the choir asked me what had happened, one of my friends said, "Aren't you lucky, you could have fallen outside Primark or Poundland".

The summer came around quite quickly again, as it seems to when you get older, and it was time to sing at the garden party. Sylvia and I set out to entertain for over an hour, and you can get through an amazing number of songs in an hour. Anyway, we had great pleasure in doing just that and we were ready for the lovely garden party. The rain hadn't stopped for days and the party could not be held in the garden, so we had the 'do' in the church. Keith and Louise had bought me a lovely red and white umbrella for Christmas – printed round the edge was, 'Singing In The Rain'. It was very useful when walking to the church in the pouring rain. We had a very good evening but on going to the back of the church when it was all over, I could not find my umbrella. I know it was something that was not very expensive but I was really disappointed when I couldn't find it. Robin was particularly upset as he tried several places to find a replacement, but to no avail. I will use a poncho next time.

At this time, our very good friend Val was suddenly feeling unwell. She had been a PE teacher and was very fit. Like our dear mutual friend, Diane, Val filled every minute of her day calling on friends, taking people to hospital and going on errands for so many people that she made my head spin. She had been having trouble with her joints and was given anti-inflammatory tablets which seemed to help for a while. She eventually had to have her knee replaced. We thought that she would soon be back to normal but we noticed that she was having trouble with her stomach. We thought that it was the anti-inflammatory tablets but unfortunately this was not the case. She had cancer in her colon, liver and lung.

We were all devastated as she was the most healthy and fit person in our circle of friends. We found out later that, like Diane, she didn't tell us the extent of her illness. We prayed for her in our Bible meetings, as did the congregation in her church. Val had many scans and consultations and it was decided that she would have surgery on her liver and then have chemotherapy over several months. The surgery took its toll on her and when we visited her she looked very weak. But she was a fighter and within a few months she was looking much better. Val has since had many treatments of chemotherapy, which she had born with great strength and determination. She is such an inspiration to us all and we are glad to have her as a friend.

Keith and Louise had the travel bug once again and asked us if we would like to join them on a trip to Canada and Alaska. Wow! The holiday 'fund piggy' came out again. We met many times to work out the itinerary, and Louise, who is so wonderfully organised, made all the arrangements. They are both very well-travelled and know how to get the best bargains. We had just over a year to get things ready and we needed all that time. We were going in the last two weeks in May and the first week in June, so decisions on what clothes to pack were not easy. Will we need snow shoes, thermal undies? We hadn't a clue what to expect.

We stayed overnight with Keith and Louise before our flight, and as before, I felt that I was in a sort of dream. I was helped onto the plane but there was so much going on that I soon forgot to be scared. We arrived in Calgary, picked up our four-by-four hire car and drove at least five hundred miles in one day to reach our first destination. We stopped at Lake Louise, which was partly frozen over and looked stunning. I stood in awe, looking at the most wonderful view with the ice melting in a sort of semi-circle, which made it look spectacular. We stayed in the most beautiful hotel in Prince Rupert and had a splendid view from our wonderful room.

We then got the ferry to go on the Inside Passage from Prince Rupert to Skagway. We were on the ferry for three days and each one was more exciting that the last. We were very fortunate to have a cabin – many young people were camping on the decks. I don't think I've ever been that brave. We saw whales, unfortunately not as close as we would have liked, but the scenery was utterly breathtaking. We stopped at Juneau and had enough time to visit the Mendenhall Glacier. A tourist behind me was very upset and I overhead her say to her tour guide, "Why is the glacier so dirty, couldn't you clean it up before the tourists come?".

We were delayed by a few hours and didn't get into Skagway until about two o'clock in the morning, but the hotel owner stayed up for us, for which we were very grateful. The hotel was a converted brothel with all the period features in each room, including the feather boas, button-up boots and other things a 'lady' would have. We were staying in Cleo's room!

Next day we picked up a large motor home and set

off for unknown territory. Our adventure was absolutely incredible and if were possible I would retrace every step of our journey. We saw grizzly bears, a wolf that was about ten feet away from us, a mother moose with her baby and incredible glaciers. If only there was a way to bottle these memories to pick up and enjoy the sensations once again! I feel so privileged to be able to say that I have seen God's creation and it is beyond description.

There was one thing that happened in Canada that touched me in a way I never dreamed of. We were in a supermarket stocking up on the usual groceries, when I came face-to-face with a young man who had only one arm. He was wearing a short sleeved T-shirt and wasn't bothered one bit. I looked at him and smiled and he recognised a fellow amputee. It made me think why couldn't I go about like that, not covering up with long sleeves? Ever since my accident I have worn jackets or cardigans, even in summer, just to hide what really was not my fault but I always thought it was. It made me think, I'm doing something wrong here. Although it did take me a little longer to actually wear short sleeves, I still have to have them covering my stump.

The choir had booked to go to Auchtermuchty – I was the only one in the choir who could pronounce it. We had such a surprise when we arrived at our accommodation. We were sharing the loveliest wooden chalets, really well appointed and warm, for which we were thankful, since it was in March. We were told on the coach that at one of our forthcoming performance venues, the original 'Doctor Finlay' was filmed in a little village nearby. From then on we were all talking like Janet, saying things like 'Arden House', and 'Ay Janet', 'Ooh Dr Cameron'. We were received so well in Scotland; I don't think the people had heard anything like our choir. We may not be the most musically disciplined, but we have been told that our faces have the Lord shining through them, which is the most important to us. Our last concert was amazing, with such a lot of young people, who whistled at us in the nicest possible way!

A few years later one of our concerts was in a Salvation Army Citadel. It was while we were waiting to rehearse that I suddenly had a strange stirring in my stomach and couldn't understand why. I was sitting in the pews and felt that I had to pick up the old hymn book in front of me. I looked for 'something', what I didn't know, but I opened the pages and I realised that I was looking at the old children's hymn, 'Jesus Loves Me'. I had been toying with the idea of making another CD, but of course it was only an idea, because there was no way that I could finance it myself, or ask anyone else to do so. But this burning in me was so strong that I felt it was from the Lord.

I shared this with Sylvia and she instantly said that she would finance it, so the wheels were set in motion. I knew I had to sing 'Jesus Loves Me' as it was obviously from the Lord. We met many times to discuss what we were going to put on the CD, who was going to produce it for us and so on. We were caught up in the excitement of it all. I asked a few people from the Celebration Choir if they would like to sing harmony in the background for me. Enid, Andrew and David were all for the idea. I contacted the producer of my original cassette, hoping that he was still doing this work and to my astonishment he remembered me. His new studio was in Chesterfield, not far from my home, so it was much easier to get there.

We were booked in for five days in March and Sylvia and I went by ourselves to start, recording test pieces to see what sounds we wanted. Listening to myself again was not what I wanted to do but it was necessary. After a very fraught five days we were satisfied with what we had done. I had to call the CD, 'Jesus Loves Me', what else? I had great fun in coming up with ideas for the cover with Craig, who is a very gifted artist and is now a graphic designer. He then designed the whole thing and I was thrilled with the finished article. The recording has been received extremely well – some of my friends from the choir were buying five at a time! I couldn't believe it.

The health of our Musical Director had been failing and we could see the pain on her face. For the first time in twenty-two years she actually sat down to conduct, which we could see was not ideal for her, and we were all so concerned. It was a shock but no surprise when it was announced that the Celebration Choir would be disbanded at the end of 2007 due to her failing health. We all thought, quite selfishly, what are we going to do now?

The next year was going to be difficult for everyone, in that we would know that each concert would be one less event for the choir and that no longer could we look forward to future concerts and booked holidays around the choir's programme. How could we possibly go on without the choir? Personally, my walk with Jesus had gone from strength to strength since singing in the choir, so I didn't want to lose that closeness with the Lord. I know that everyone's walk is so different, but music is my walk. I can sing every song I choose to sing with such feeling, knowing that it could only come from Him.

I knew that Sylvia and I could still entertain at the

nursing homes and other venues. But although we always include some Christian songs at every venue, whether or not the audience are believers, we still felt that this might not be enough to fulfil our sense of being near to the Lord.

After each concert that followed the announcement of disbandment, we would discuss how we would get through our final concert without there being tears on every face. The dreaded last concert came around all too quickly. It was to be held in the Octagon Centre, near Sheffield University. There was a pre-concert report in the evening paper and the event was a sellout.

It was an amazing evening. Many ex-choir members turned up and it was just like a great reunion. We sang our last song. It seemed to go so fast, and then it was all over. We had made so many friends, good friends, and it was heart-breaking to say goodbye.

In the meantime Gilbert had retired and very naughtily I thought if I was going to cope with him under my feet all day, I hoped that he wouldn't object to me going out with Sylvia during the day, entertaining. Much to my surprise it has actually been rather good, as we can check the weather in the morning and zip off to the coast – more often than not to Whitby, which is one of our favourite places. I often think of the early years of our marriage and that if it had been the way it is now, how different life could have been. But then I wouldn't have had all the wonderful experiences, good and bad, to compare with my life now.

Chapter 6

I was having difficulty with my hand, especially my thumb, which was rather painful and making life just a tad difficult. I couldn't grip anything, which made opening bottles and jars a bit awkward and I had to depend on either Gilbert or Craig. I went to see the doctor and I was sent again to the hospital. The physiotherapist gave me a course of injections that I hoped would work, but unfortunately after the third one I had to go back and start the process all over again. Fortunately I didn't have to wait too long for surgery as the consultant was able to fit me into his schedule quite quickly. The operation was set for the 16th of December – what is it about December and every two years? Unfortunately we had to cancel several singing engagements, two of which were our favourites. There was one that we have been to for many years, where the church is lit only by candles and the atmosphere is peaceful, serene and soothing.

I had the operation as a day patient, going in at eight o'clock in the morning and out in the afternoon, which seems straightforward but after a general anaesthetic this earth or Fuller's come into play. Gilbert collected me and then it suddenly hit me that I couldn't open the car door, or anything else, because I had a plaster cast from my knuckles to my elbow. My arm was completely numb and it sort of flopped about, so everything was a struggle. Again, everyone was wonderful, doing things for me, but having been fiercely independent all my life it was difficult to deal with.

I didn't tell Mum, as she was now ninety three and still worried about her children, especially her youngest 'wean'. I knew she would have been distraught to know I was going through more surgery. I normally telephone her at six o'clock every evening and I had to keep everything as normal as possible, trying to sound cheery and pain free. I convinced her that all was well, even though Gilbert had to hold the phone up to my ear. As soon as I put the telephone down I took the pain killers, although sometimes I thought that two Smarties would have been just as effective.

Keith and Louise had decided to buy a boat. It was built in Holland and would be moored there. We were shown the photos of the various stages as it was being built. We were invited to have a holiday in the boat and never having been to Holland, Gilbert and I jumped at the chance. So off we trotted to the Netherlands and we met some wonderful people. Did you know that the Dutch kiss you three times on the cheeks? On board I resisted the temptation to say things like 'shiver me timbers' and 'hang him from the yard arm'. Sailing on the canals in Holland was a lovely experience and the little villages at the side of the water were beautiful. I sat at the 'pointed end' just soaking up the peace and calm, not to mention the sunshine. The boat was beautifully appointed and was very spacious, and Louise and I managed to work very well together in the 'galley'.

During the year of the choir's disbandment, Sylvia and I talked for hours about starting a new choir. We knew that it would not be as simple as gathering a group of people together and saying, "Now sing!". We tried to keep it quiet because we did not really want a very large choir and we feared that, if everyone knew, we would have at least a hundred singers and we just couldn't cope with that many. So at the last choir concert we asked people who lived within striking distance of Dronfield if they would like to join another choir. The response was remarkable and before we knew it, we had a new choir, the logistics of which we still had not thought about. We were to have a last choir meeting with everyone just before Christmas, a wonderful buffet, great company and a chance to meet everyone who wanted to join us in our new venture.

We hadn't a clue as to who would be our Musical Director, Treasurer or Secretary, but God did and soon volunteers came forward. It confirmed our belief that it was right to start up again. We held a meeting in January. About eighty people turned up and we knew who was going to stay or not. We decided to give ourselves a year to see if we would be invited to sing anywhere, and if we felt that it wasn't working, we would give up. Well, we needn't have worried, as we started rehearsals in February and aimed for the first concert in July. We thought it would take a long time before we would all gel together, but the Lord had other plans and we just seemed to fit together.

Why are we always surprised when the Lord answers our prayers? We shouldn't be, but we are. The new choir was a great success and we took many bookings. It was difficult not to compare the new choir with the old, but the Celebration Choir had been so unique that it was impossible to replicate it; we had to be different. We sang with the Salvation Army Band at a Christmas concert. The atmosphere was wonderful and we were booked for the following year. The Celebration Choir had not done a

Christmas concert and so we looked forward to singing the wonderful carols in four-part harmony.

Music has been such a huge influence in my life that I cannot easily understand how others could not share the joy that it brings me. Gilbert does not listen to music voluntarily, even in the car, so it's me who has the radio turned up loud. I have every one of Enya's CDs and I know he likes these. Craig's bedroom is right above the kitchen and I bet I'm the only mum whose son asks her to turn the music down!

Our new choir has been much more successful than we could possibly have imagined and we are consistently booked up, eighteen months ahead. So, the Lord has His hand in what we are doing. We all pray that it will continue to have a successful future. Apart from the wonderful music, the fellowship in the choir has been uplifting and touching; so much so, that when any choir member has a problem, there will be fifty friends supporting and praying for them.

The time came around again for us to sing at the Garden Party and we were lucky to have a beautiful sunny day. There was a superb jazz band playing and Sylvia and I strolled through garden, listening to the terrific music. We sat on an available bench, leaned back and the legs of the bench slowly disappeared into the soil, tipping us up in what it seemed like a slow motion film. We had to ask two strong men to haul us up. It was less than dignified and the only way we saved our blushes was that almost everyone was admiring my new red shoes. When it was my time to go to the microphone the only thing I could say was, "For those who missed our warm-up act, I shall not be repeating it – thank you very much". I also realised why that bench was so readily available.

I'm so pleased that both my children have inherited my love of every type of music. Adele must have at least six hundred CDs; some I recognise and some that are so obscure that I'm sure she's made up the names of the bands herself. Craig's love of music is very eclectic too and I've often said to him when he is sitting at his computer that it sometimes sounds like psychological warfare.

Earlier in this story I mentioned Adele's fear of spiders. She does a lot of shift work as a paramedic and sees some terrible sights. She doesn't often tell me the detail of the accidents she has to attend, but she did tell me of three horrendous incidents that I found difficult to believe that my daughter could cope with. After describing one of these bad road accidents and what she had done to help the poor souls involved, she said that she had been in her greenhouse and saw a huge spider – totally terrified, she screamed and ran out as fast as she could!

As I come to the end of this story, I have to make some additions. Our dear friend Val lost her long battle with cancer. For four and a half years she looked so well, dressed beautifully and always wore her make-up, doing the things that she always had done, mostly for other people. She hadn't told us just how ill she was, and it was such a shock to us all that she suddenly seemed to be so ill, so quickly. Sylvia and I went to visit her in hospital and on one occasion she looked especially poorly but our spirits were lifted when she looked much better on the next visit. We visited her in the hospice where she looked much more comfortable, but on my last visit I knew my dear friend was going to be with her Lord. It was with a heavy heart that I received the phone call I had dreaded. It brought back many memories of my other dear friend Diane, who had played badminton and squash with Val while I looked on. I know neither of them ever said, "Why me?". Their faith was strong and now they are singing joyful praises in Heaven.

How could my life have turned out this way? I think that I have been able to put all the problems and fears behind me because I have the love of Jesus in my life. On looking back, I believe that He was in my life long before I knew Him. He has helped me through so many events, dramas, traumas and, of course, stage fright. Apart from singing in the choir, Sylvia and I still go and entertain and we are asked to many more places, which we both love. We have met many wonderful people, some Christian and some not, but no matter where we entertain we always sing some Christian songs, of which there are many beautiful modern ones. I still love my life. I know that I will soon be visiting the good old NHS again, as now most of the knuckles and joints of my wrist and hand are wearing out. My dear husband still says that I'm lucky that my tongue hasn't worn out, but Craig has now decided that I have something that he calls 'UGS', which translates as 'Unnecessary Gesticulation Syndrome'. He often asks me to try to talk with my hand in my pocket – impossible.

Gilbert and I celebrated our fortieth wedding anniversary and our children decided that we should do something very special, suggesting that we try an all-inclusive holiday in the Dominican Republic. We had not been on holiday as a couple before and I thought that it would be easy as we went into town and booked the holiday in the Caribbean. There was only one problem with the plan, and I thought of it only after we had paid, that it involved a ten hour flight. More pills from the good doctor.

We had an amazing time and the people we met,

especially the waiters and waitresses, were extremely kind and thoughtful. We saw how the world is very ill-divided, as the poverty we witnessed was absolutely heartbreaking, but the children seemed to be unaware that they were poor. It brought home to me how poor I thought we were when I was a child, but nothing that I suffered came close to what we saw. However, we were aware beforehand of what we might see and I didn't let these sights spoil my holiday, but it still makes me feel so grateful for what the Lord has provided for me and my family.

I have tried to remember, as best I can, how my life has been. I know that my memories will not be the same as those of my brother or sisters, as there are a quite a few years between us, so my apologies to them. I have had a wonderful life in spite of the ups and downs, and have had the love of a family who have helped me through many traumas. I have been blessed with many wonderful friends and through everything the love of Jesus has made my life whole.